beyond
tic tac toe

Challenging and exciting new games to be
played with colored pens or pencils

by Sid Sackson /Pantheon Books

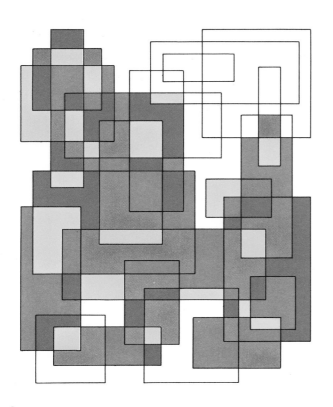

Games mean many things to many people; to me they are an art form of great potential beauty. Just as a composer's creation is brought to life by the performing musicians, a game inventor's creation is brought to life by the players of the game. When the creation is inspired and the players are talented, a true work of art results.

In creating the seven games in this book I have attempted to add a new visual dimension to the art of games. As each is played, a colorful drawing is formed. Because these drawings are reminiscent in style of the works of different modern masters of abstract art—some well known, others not so well —I have named the games in honor of the artists.

Eight removable sheets are provided for six of the games; sixteen for the fastest game—SPRINGER. Each sheet is used for one match. The only other equipment required are colored pencils (or crayons, or magic markers, or you name it) of two to four colors, depending on the game chosen and the number of players.

S.S.

VASARELY

Victor Vasarely, b. Hungary, 1908

The playing field is divided by heavy lines into ten *cubes* and each cube is divided by light lines into *spaces,* varying from seven to twelves in a cube. Each space is identified by the number of dots—one to five—it contains.

The areas in the four corners of the sheet are for keeping score. Each player uses one area and writes his initials in the box marked X. As he gains points he colors in one small box for each point. At the end of the game his total score is entered in the box marked T.

The Play. Each player uses a different color. The first player is chosen in any convenient manner. He picks any cube and fills in a one-dot space in that cube with his color. The player to the left now fills in a two-dot space, either in the same cube or in a second cube of his choice. No more than two cubes may be in play at one time. Once two cubes have been picked, all the spaces in one of them must be filled before a new cube is picked by a subsequent player.

The players, in turn to the left, fill spaces in the following sequence: one-dot, two-dot, three-dot, four-dot, five-dot, one-dot, two-dot, etc. If a space containing a player's required number appears in only one of the two cubes in play, he must use that cube. If neither cube contains a space of his required number, he does not fill in any space on that turn.

When a player fills in the last space in a cube, he scores one point for each space in that cube with a color *other* than his

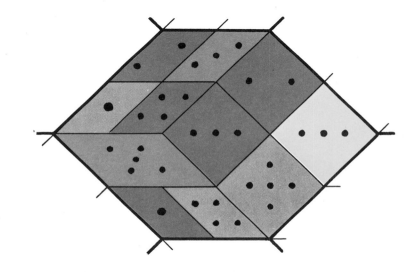

own. [For example, in the illustration the red player completes a cube in which three spaces are red, two are blue, one is yellow, and five are green. He scores eight points.] When all ten cubes have been completed, the game is over and the player with the highest total is the winner.

Variation. For a much more difficult game, allow up to three cubes to be in play at one time.

MIRO

Joan Miró, b. Spain, 1893

The playing field consists of a continuous line that crosses and recrosses itself forming 109 *spaces* of different shapes. The line between two crossing points is called a *segment*. There are 209 segments.

At each end of the sheet are two areas for keeping score. When three or four play, each uses one area and writes his initials in the box marked X. When four play, each may play for himself or teams may be formed with partners sitting diagonally opposite each other. When two play, each uses two areas. As a player gains points, he colors in one small box for each point. At the end of the game his total score is entered in the box marked T.

The Play. Each player uses a different color. The first player is determined in any convenient manner. He chooses one segment and covers it with his color. [See A in Illustration 1, showing a sample game played by two players on a mini-field.] The player to the left must now cover with his color two continuous segments along the curve at either end of the original segment. [See B in Illustration 1. The segments could, if desired, have been colored from the right end of A.] The next player to the left must now color three continuous segments along the curve from the two segments just colored. [See C in Illustration 1.] The players, in turn to the left, continue along the curve from the last segment colored, but now have a choice between coloring either one, two, or three continuous segments. [In Illustration 1, the blue player chooses to color three segments—D. The red player chooses to color only one segment—E. The blue player now chooses to color two segments—F.]

When a player colors a segment that completes the surrounding of a space, he captures that space and scores one point for each segment of his own color that surrounds the space. More than one space may be captured by a player on his turn.

Illustration 1

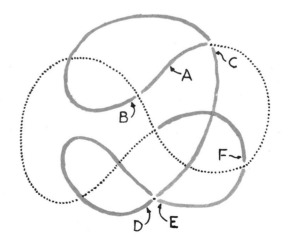

[In Illustration 2, the red player captures two spaces with G, each being worth one point. In Illustration 3, the blue player captures four spaces with H. For the purposes of this diagram, point values are indicated by the number of dots in each space. The red player finishes the mini-game by capturing five spaces with I.]

When all the segments have been colored and all the spaces have been captured, the game is over. The player with the highest number of points wins. [In the illustrated mini-game, the red player wins with fourteen points to the blue player's ten.] If four are playing in teams, partners add their scores and the team with the highest total wins.

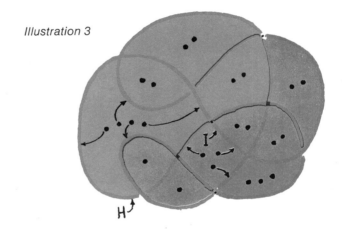

Illustration 3

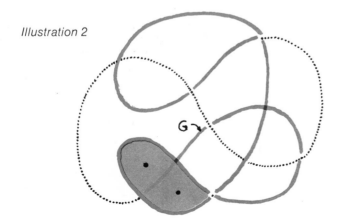

Illustration 2

Variations for Scoring in Partnership Play. (1) At the end of the game, the player in each team with the *lower* number of points doubles his score. (If both players in a team have the same number of points, double either one.) This is then added to his partner's score to determine the team total. Play is the same as in the standard game, but partners should plan their strategy to keep both scores as even as possible. (2) At the end of the game, the player in each team with the *higher* number of points doubles his score. This is then added to his partner's score to determine the team's total. Play is the same as in the standard game, but partners should plan their strategy to favor the leading player as much as possible.

MONDRIAN

Piet Mondrian, b. Holland, 1872

2, 3, or 4 players

The playing field consists of ninety-nine *spaces* of different shapes and sizes.

At each end of the sheet are two areas for keeping score. Each player uses one area and writes his initials in the box marked X. As he gains points he colors one small box for each point scored. At the end of the game his total score is entered in the box marked T. When four play, each may play for himself or teams may be formed with partners sitting diagonally opposite each other.

The Play for Four. Each player uses a different color. The first player is chosen in any convenient manner. He picks any space on the playing field and fills it with his color. The player to his left then fills in a space next to the first space. Touching at a corner is not considered "next to." Each player, in turn to the left, fills in a space next to one or more previously colored spaces—but not necessarily the one just colored. A player may never fill in a space next to one he has already colored.

When a player fills in a space that completes a *rectangle* of two or more spaces, he scores as many points as there are spaces in the completed rectangle. If he completes two or more rectangles at the same time, he scores only the one with the higher number of spaces.

[Illustration 1 shows a game in progress on a mini-field with thirteen spaces. The red player is first and picks space A. Yellow plays second and fills space B, which is next to space A. Blue

plays third and fills space C. He has completed a rectangle consisting of spaces B and C and scores two points. Green now fills space D and scores two points for the rectangle consisting

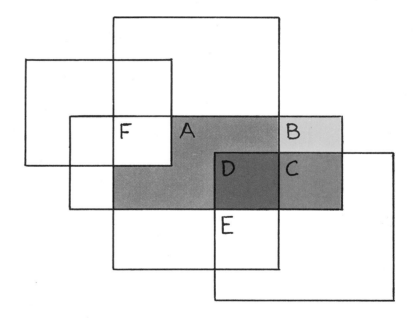

Illustration 1

of spaces C and D. The red player would like to fill space F, but it is next to space A which is already red. Instead red fills space E—see Illustration 2—and scores two points for rectangle D,E. Yellow plays next and fills space F. He scores five points for rectangle A,B,C,D,F. A rectangle consisting of spaces A,D,F

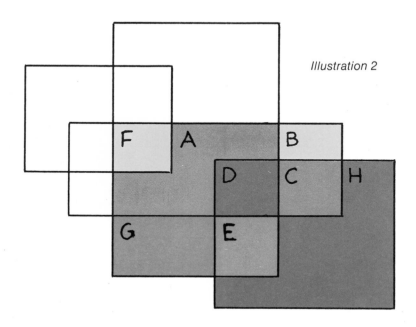

Illustration 2

was also completed, but it has fewer spaces and therefore is not scored. Blue fills space G and scores five points for rectangle A,D,E,F,G. Green fills space H, scoring four points for rectangle C,D,E,H.]

The game ends when one player fills his scoring area—eighty points. If no player reaches eighty points before the playing field is completed, the player with the highest score wins. Some spaces may remain unfilled because they are next to all four colors. When four are playing in teams, the individual scores of the partners are added (even if one has reached eighty points) and the higher total wins.

The Play for Three. Each player uses a different color. A fourth color is *neutral,* meaning that any player may use it. On his turn, a player may use the neutral color instead of his own. The neutral color may not be filled in next to itself. If a player completes a rectangle with the neutral color, he does not score (but he may use this play to stop an opponent from completing a high-scoring rectangle). All other rules are the same as in the play for four.

The Play for Two. Each player uses a different color. A third color is neutral. Instead of ending the game when a player reaches eighty points, the players may agree in advance to play to 160 points, each using two scoring areas. All other rules are the same as in the play for three and four.

ARP

Hans Arp, b. Germany, 1887

The playing field consists of twenty-five straight *lines* that cross each other to form fifty-five *spaces*. At each end of the sheet are two areas for keeping score. Each player uses one area and writes his initials in the box marked X. As he gains points he colors in one small box for each point. When four play, each may play for himself or teams may be formed with partners sitting diagonally opposite each other.

The Play. Each player uses a different color. The first player is determined in any convenient manner. He chooses any of the straight lines and covers its entire length with his color. The player to his left then chooses a line that touches the previously colored line and colors it from the point where it touches to its end. If the line chosen crosses the line just colored, the player may choose the direction he will take, but may not color it in both directions. Players, in turn to the left, choose a line that touches the line *just* colored and color it in one direction until the end, or until a portion previously colored is reached.

On a player's turn, if no uncolored line touches the line just colored, the player chooses any remaining uncolored line and colors its entire length.

When a player's line completes the surrounding of a space (third side of a triangle, fourth side of a quadrilateral, etc.) he fills in that space with his color and scores one point. More than one space may be captured by a player on his turn.

[Illustration 1 shows a game in progress on a mini-field with

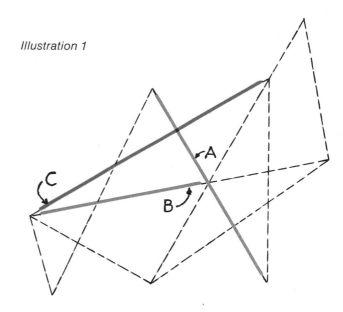

Illustration 1

thirteen spaces. The red player begins the game by coloring the entire length of line A. Blue follows by choosing line B. And green chooses line C. In Illustration 2, red colors line D, capturing a space. Blue then colors line E—the only uncolored line touching the line just colored—and captures two spaces. Green colors line F, capturing one space. And red colors line G, also capturing one space. There is now no uncolored line that touches G. Blue may choose to color any one of the six lines marked H. He chooses the one shown in Illustration 3, capturing one space. Green follows with line I, also capturing one space. Red continues with line J, again capturing one space.]

When all the lines have been colored and all the spaces have been captured, the game ends. The player with the highest number of points wins. If played with partners, the higher team total wins.

Illustration 3

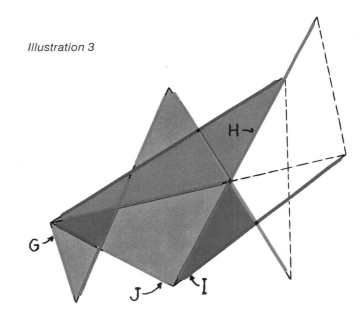

Illustration 2

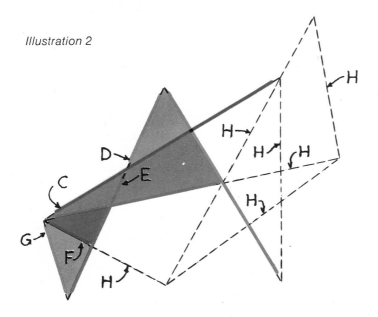

Variation. (1) When coloring a line, a player stops upon reaching a line he has already covered. [In Illustration 2, the blue line E would be stopped by the existing blue line. And in Illustration 3, the blue line H may run in either direction from the existing blue line, but may not run past it.] (2) The "Variations for Scoring in Partnership Play" given with MIRO may also be used.

DELAUNEY

Sonia Delaunay, b. Russia, 1885   *Robert Delaunay, b. France, 1885*

The playing field is divided by heavy lines into nine *sections.* Each section is divided by dotted lines into *spaces,* varying from nineteen to twenty-four in a section. At one end of the sheet are three rows of boxes for keeping score. When two or three play, each writes his initials in a box marked X. When a player *loses* a point he colors in a small box in the row next to his initials. When four play, teams are formed—with partners sitting diagonally opposite each other—and partners use the same row for scoring.

The Play for Four. Each player uses a different color. Determine the first player in any convenient manner. He chooses a space in any section of the playing field and fills it in with his color. Play continues in this section until it is completed. Each player, in turn to the left, fills in a space next to one or more previously colored spaces—not necessarily the one just colored. A player may never fill in a space next to one that he has already colored.

Each time a player is unable to fill in a space in the section in play, he must fill in a box in his team's scoring row, indicating the loss of a point. Play continues, with some players filling in spaces while others mark off scoring boxes, until a player fills in the last available space. One or more spaces may remain empty because they are next to all four colors. The other three players now mark off scoring boxes and the section is completed.

[Illustration 1 shows a game in progress in one section of a

mini-field. The red and yellow players are partners against blue and green. Red is chosen to play first and picks space A. Blue follows with space B. Play continues in this manner until green

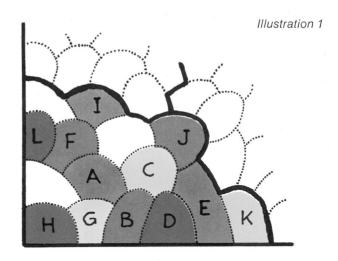

Illustration 1

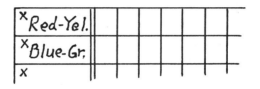

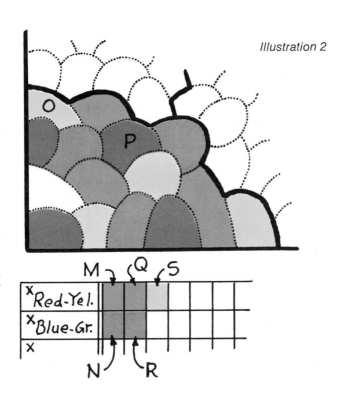

Illustration 2

O and green follows with space P—the last space that can be filled. Red, blue, and yellow now mark off scoring boxes Q,R, and S, completing the section.]

The player who colors the last space in the completed section [green in the illustrated game] picks any one of the remaining sections and fills in any space. Play continues as before, with each player filling in a space next to one or more spaces previously colored in this section. When a space that borders on a previously completed section is filled in, it may not be next to a space of the same color in that section. When all nine sections have been completed, the game ends and the team with the *lowest* score wins.

The Play for Three. Play is the same as the standard game, except that each player plays for himself.

The Play for Two. Play is the same as the standard game, except that each player uses two different colors, for a total of four colors in the game. On his turn a player may use either one of his colors to fill in a space. When, on his turn, a player is unable to fill in a space with either color, he must mark off a box in his scoring row.

fills in space L and each player has colored three spaces. Red is unable to fill in a space and marks off a scoring box—M. See Illustration 2. Blue marks off scoring box N. Yellow fills in space

KLEE

Paul Klee, b. Switzerland, 1879

The playing field consists of 144 *spaces*. Around the field is a scoring track. The players write their initials on either side of the arrow at the start of the track, and mark off their points along the track as scored. At either end of the sheet are six *areas* for placing *scoring sequences*—one side for each player. For the standard game, only the four areas between the asterisks are used. Experienced players may agree in advance to use all six areas.

The Set Up. Four colors are used, but unlike the previous games no color belongs to a player. The first player (chosen in any convenient manner) selects three colors to make up his first scoring sequence. He then fills in his first area, beginning at the left, with his chosen colors. The second player now fills in his first area. He may use the same colors but may not duplicate the sequence used by the first player. [For example, if the first player chooses ▨▨▨ the second player may not choose either ▨▨▨ or ▨▨▨ . He may, however, choose ▨▨▨ or ▨▨▨ etc.] The first player now chooses a second scoring sequence and fills in his second area accordingly. He may not use the same three colors as in his first sequence but must instead introduce the fourth color, dropping one of the others. He may not duplicate his opponent's sequence. The second player similarly fills in his second area.

The first player fills in his third area with any *two* colors, the end spaces being the same color. The second player—as always

—may not duplicate his opponent's sequence. The first player finishes by using two colors in his fourth area. He may not use the same two colors as in his third area, but may, if he wishes, use one of them. [For example, if he used ▨▨▨ for his third box, he could not choose ▨▨▨ for his fourth. He could, however, choose ▨▨▨ or ▨▨▨ etc.] The second player similarly fills in his fourth area. [Illustration 1 shows one of the many possible set ups of the four areas.]

Illustration 1

The Play. The first player chooses a space in the playing field and fills it in with any color he wishes. The second player then fills in a space that touches the first space, either along an edge or at a corner. He may also use any color he wishes. Players, in turn, use any color to fill in a space that touches one or more of the previously colored spaces—not necessarily the space just colored.

When a player succeeds in forming one of his scoring sequences on the playing field—in any direction, including diagonally—he scores one point. If other scoring sequences are formed at the same time, or the same sequence is formed in different positions, the player scores one point for each. [By filling in the space indicated with a green circle in Illustration 2, a player with the set up shown in Illustration 1 would score six points for forming the following sequences: in line A; in lines B and C; in line D; and

 in lines E and F.] If a player forms one of his opponent's scoring sequences, it is disregarded.

A player wins by being the first to reach the end of the scoring track. For a shorter game, the players may cut off the scoring track at any point agreed to in advance. A player also wins if at any time he is at least *five points* ahead of his opponent. If the playing field is filled before a player wins in either of the above ways, the player in the lead is the winner.

Variation. When a player forms more than one scoring sequence at a time, he scores in accordance with the following table: 2 sequences = 3 points; 3 sequences = 6 points; 4 sequences = 10 points; 5 sequences = 15 points; 6 sequences = 21 points; 7 sequences = 28 points; 8 sequences = 36 points.

With this variation, the rule that a player wins by being at least five points ahead of his opponent is not used.

Illustration 2

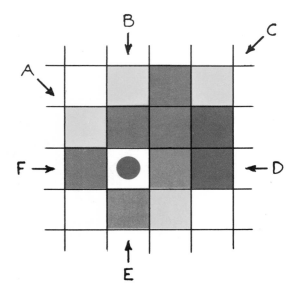

SPRINGER

Ferdinand Springer, b. Germany, 1907

2, 3, or 4 players

The playing field consists of a large rectangle divided into 108 *spaces* of different shapes and sizes. Connected to each edge of the large rectangle are *triangles* marked with numbers from one to five.

The Play for Two. Each player uses a different color. The first player is chosen in any convenient manner. He picks a space and fills it with his color. The other player then picks a space anywhere on the playing field and fills it with his color. Play continues in this manner with the exception that a player may never fill in a space next to one that already has his color. Touching at a corner is not considered "next to." [In the illustration, which shows only the spaces chosen by one player, red may not fill in any of the spaces marked X.]

Instead of filling in a space, a player may, on his turn, fill in a numbered triangle. Each player may fill in only one triangle on each of the four edges of the playing field. [In the illustration, red may not fill in another triangle along any of the three edges shown.]

Each player tries to form a *chain* of his color—spaces connected to each other at their corners and connected to triangles on all four edges of the playing field. The four triangles must total thirteen or more. [In the illustration, a red chain is shown connected to triangles on three edges, with a total of nine. To win, the red player would have to connect to a triangle on the fourth edge containing either a four or a five.]

When a player completes a chain to all four edges with a total of thirteen or more, the game ends—except, if the player who originally played first completes, the second player has one final turn. If only one player completes a chain, he is the winner. If both complete chains, the one with the higher total wins. If the totals are the same, the game is a draw. If neither player

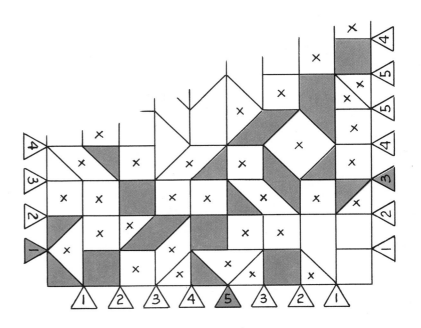

is able to complete a chain, each player totals the triangles he has connected to, and the higher total wins.

The Play for Three or Four. The rules are the same as for two players, except that a player wins by connecting to one triangle on each of the four edges, regardless of their total. (Usually, however, no player will complete a chain to all four edges and the winner will be determined by the highest total of triangles connected to.)

Variations for Two Experienced Players. (1) Instead of totalling thirteen for a winning chain, the total may be lowered for a faster game or raised for a tighter game. (2) Before the start of the game, each player—using black ink or pencil—divides a space of his choice into two spaces, making a total of 110 spaces. (3) On his first turn each player fills in two spaces that are next to each other, making them into one space. (4) The variations above may be combined, either two at a time or all three together.

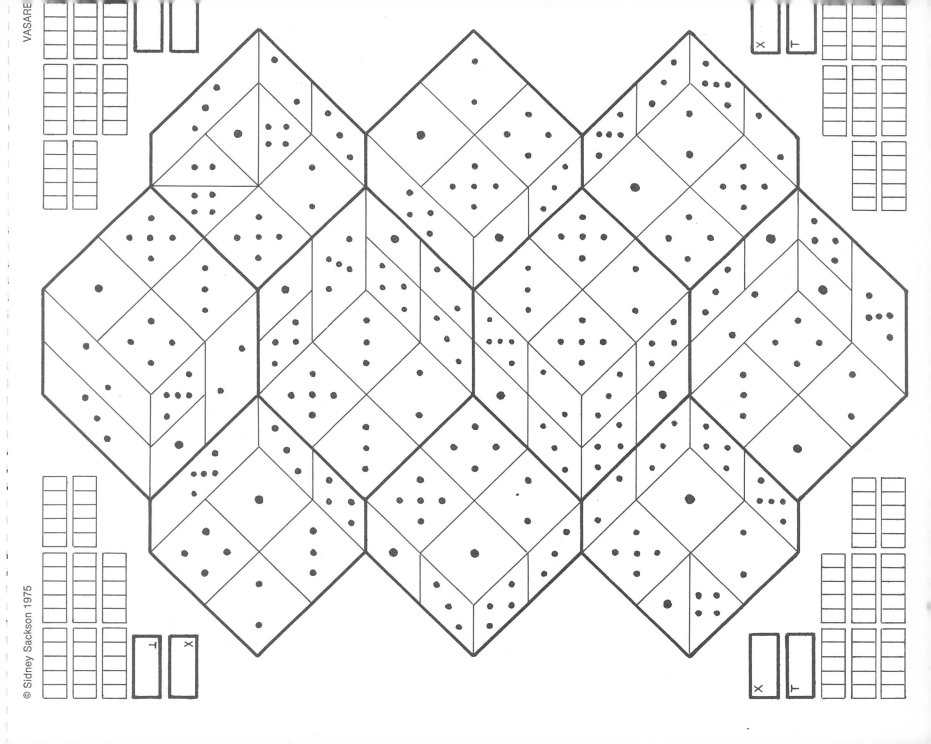

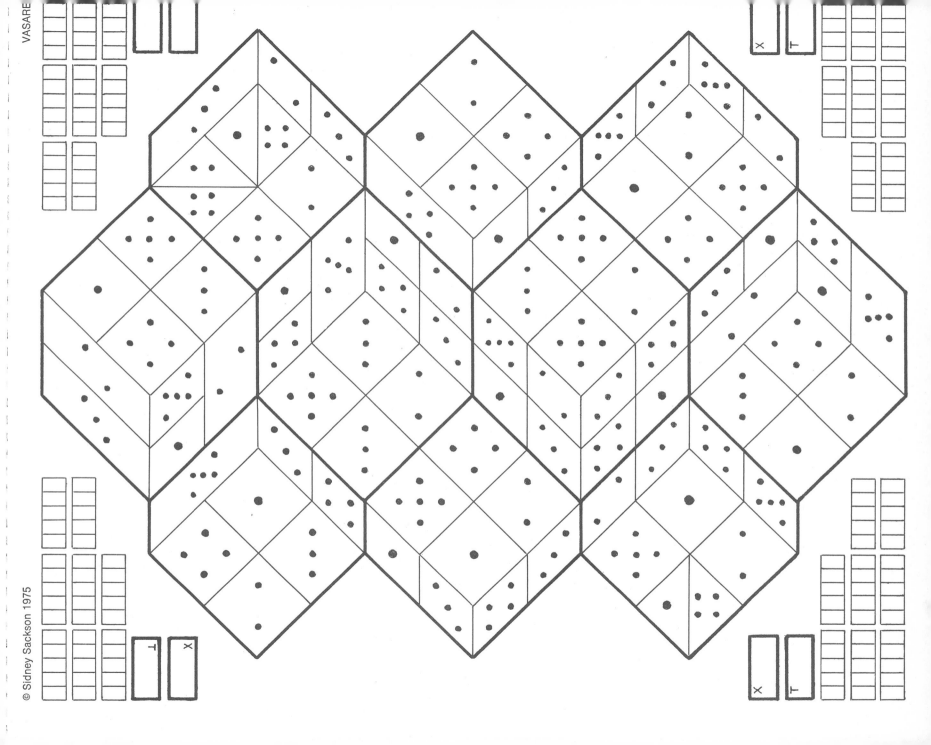

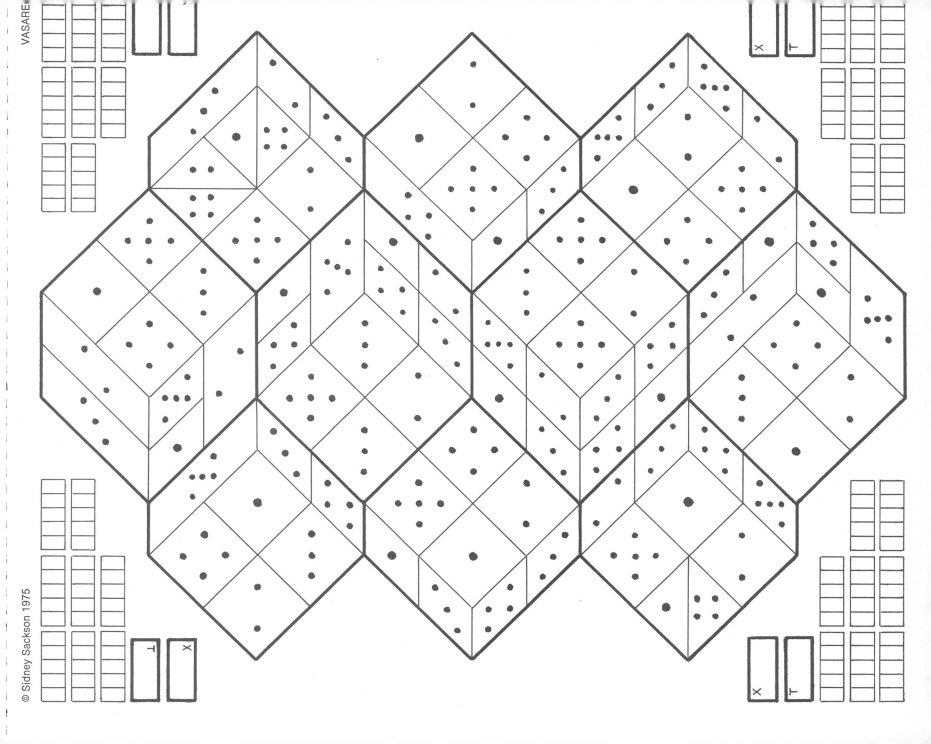

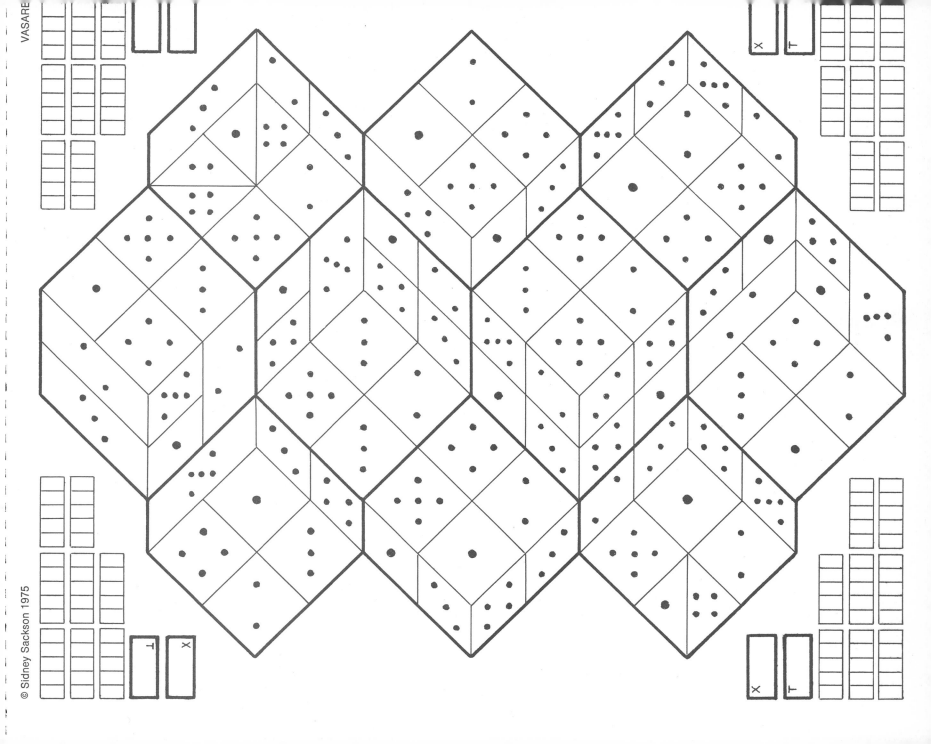

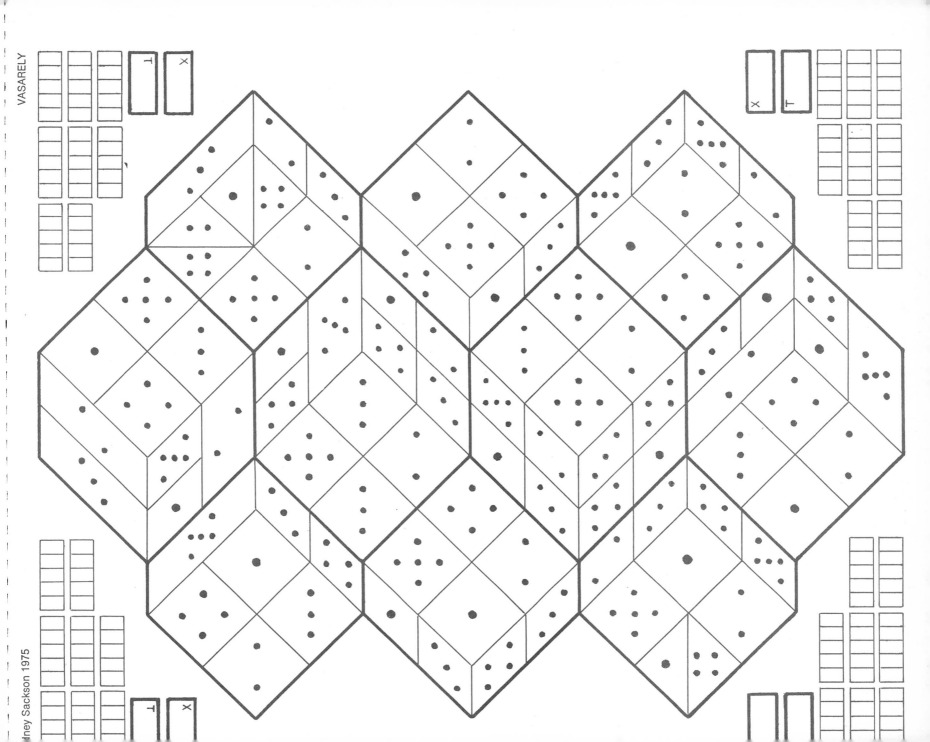

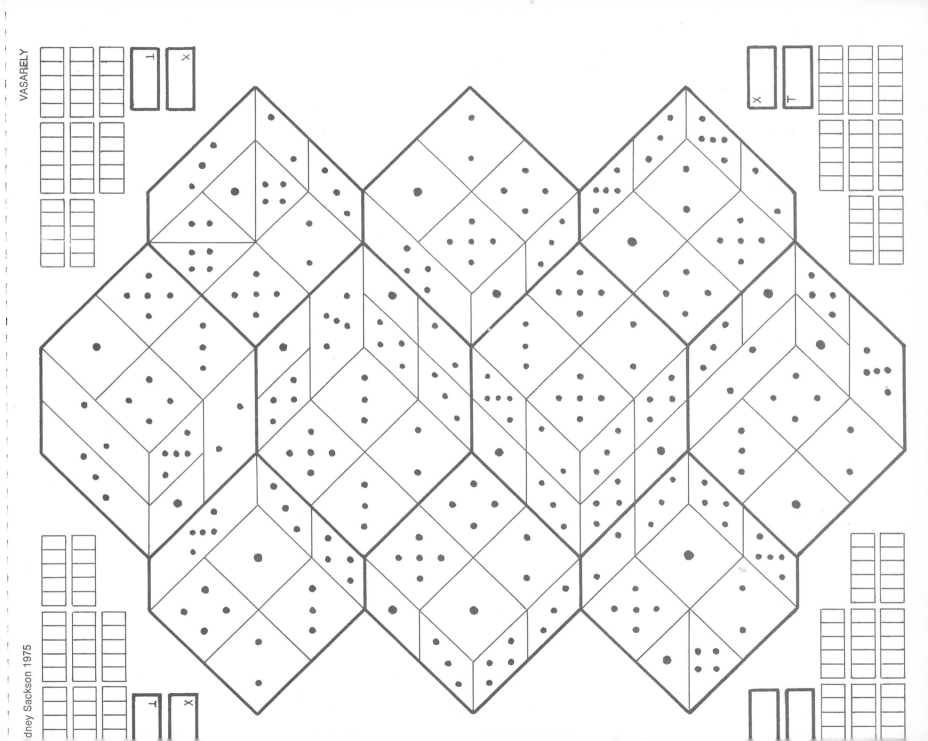

VASARELY

Sidney Sackson 1975

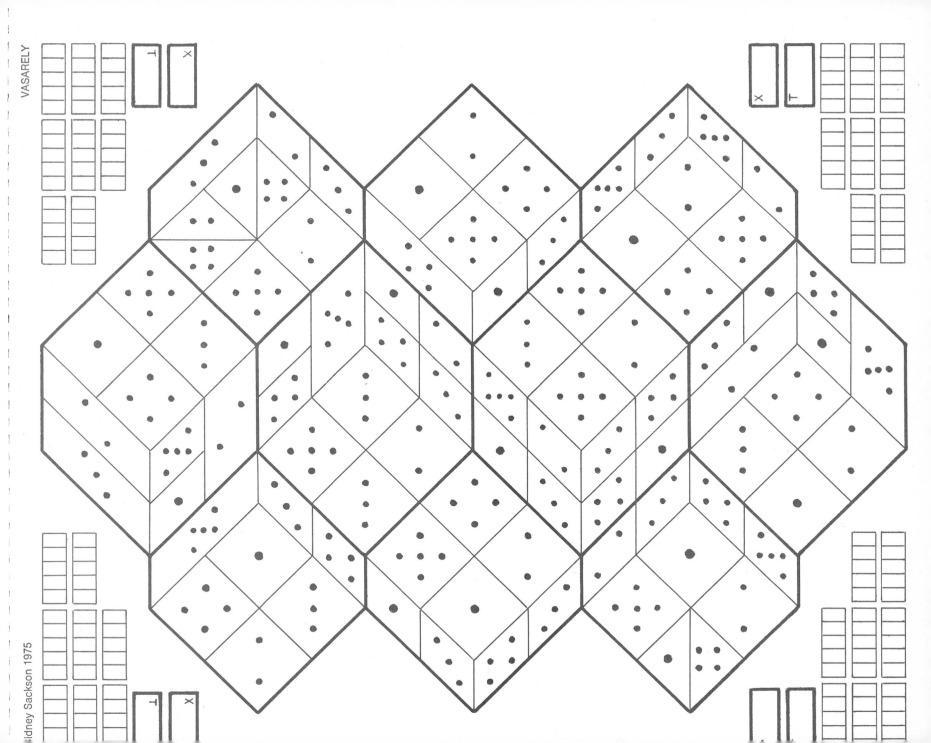

Sidney Sackson 1975

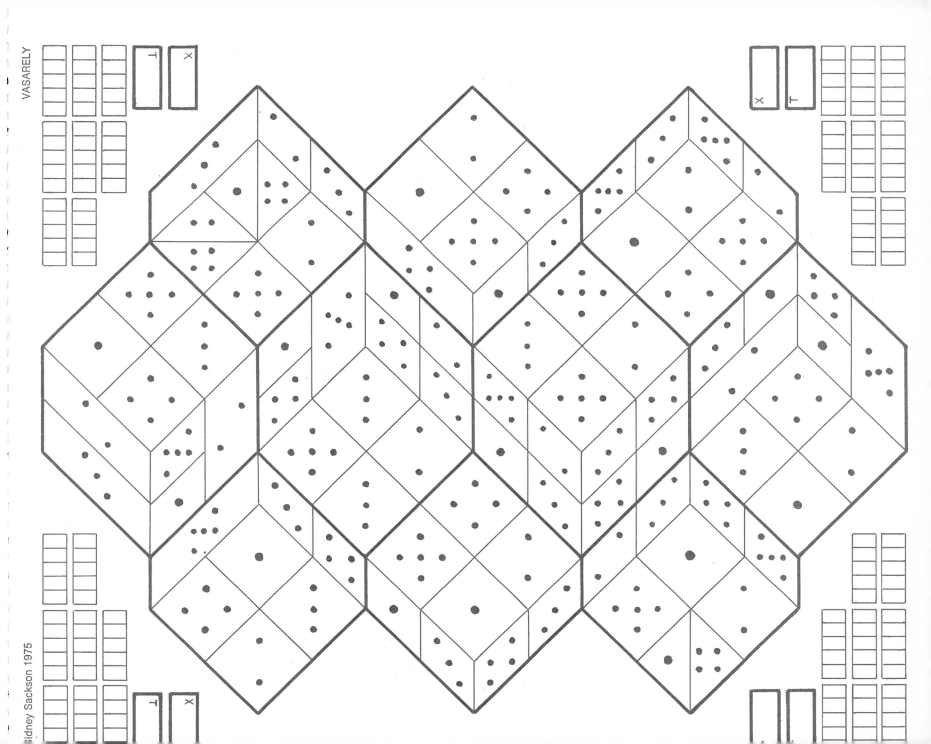

Sidney Sackson 1975

MIRO

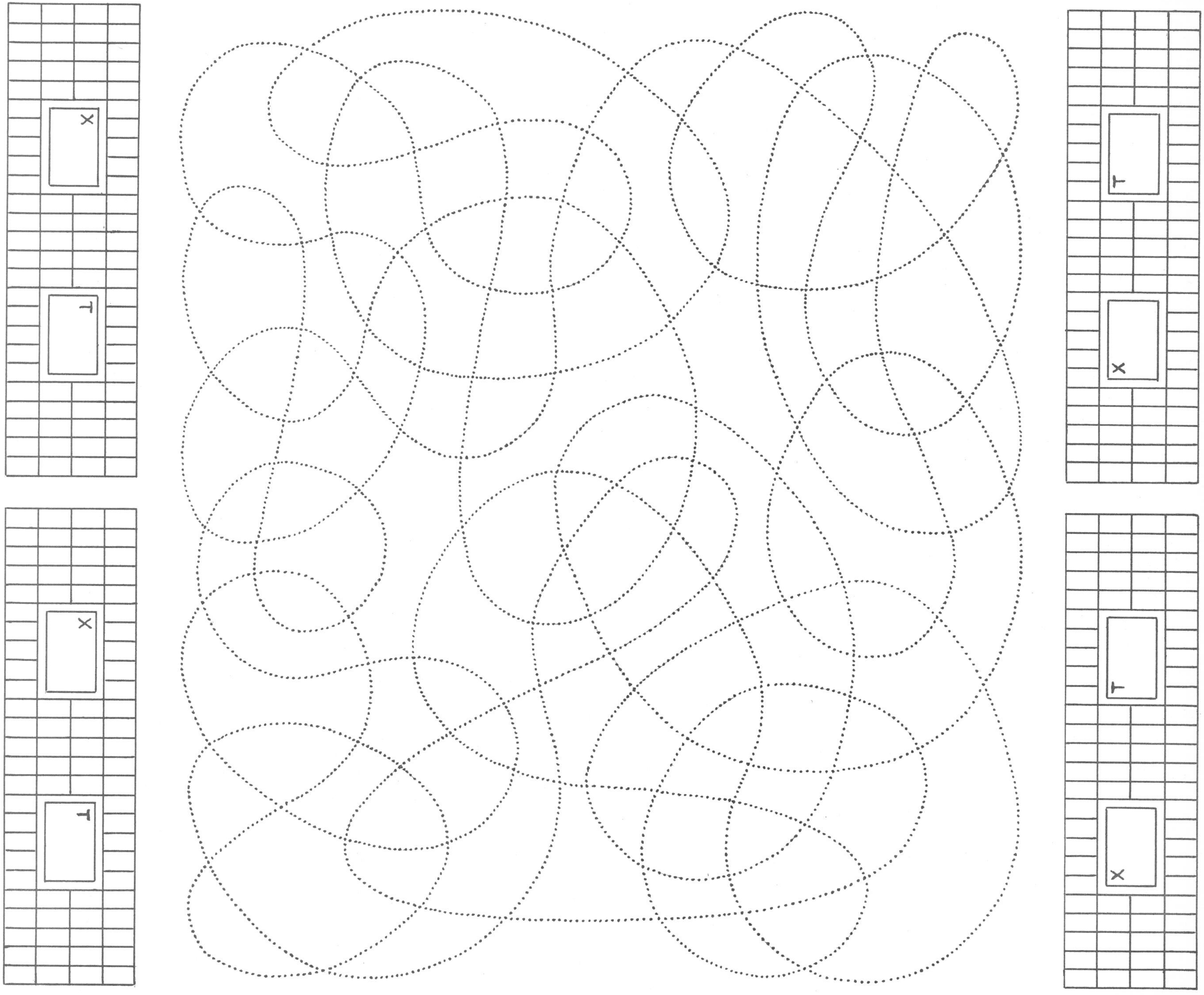

MIRO

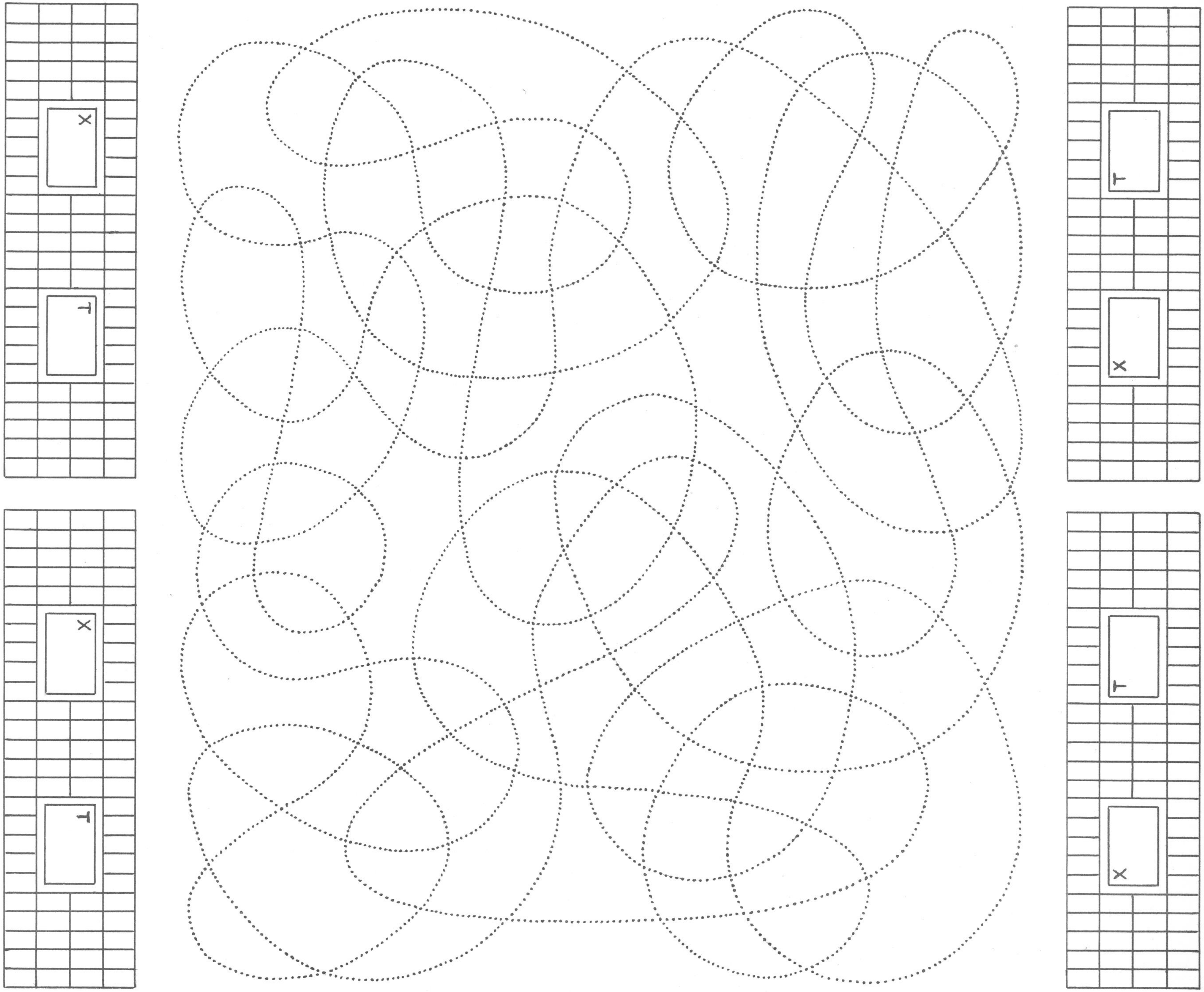

MIRO

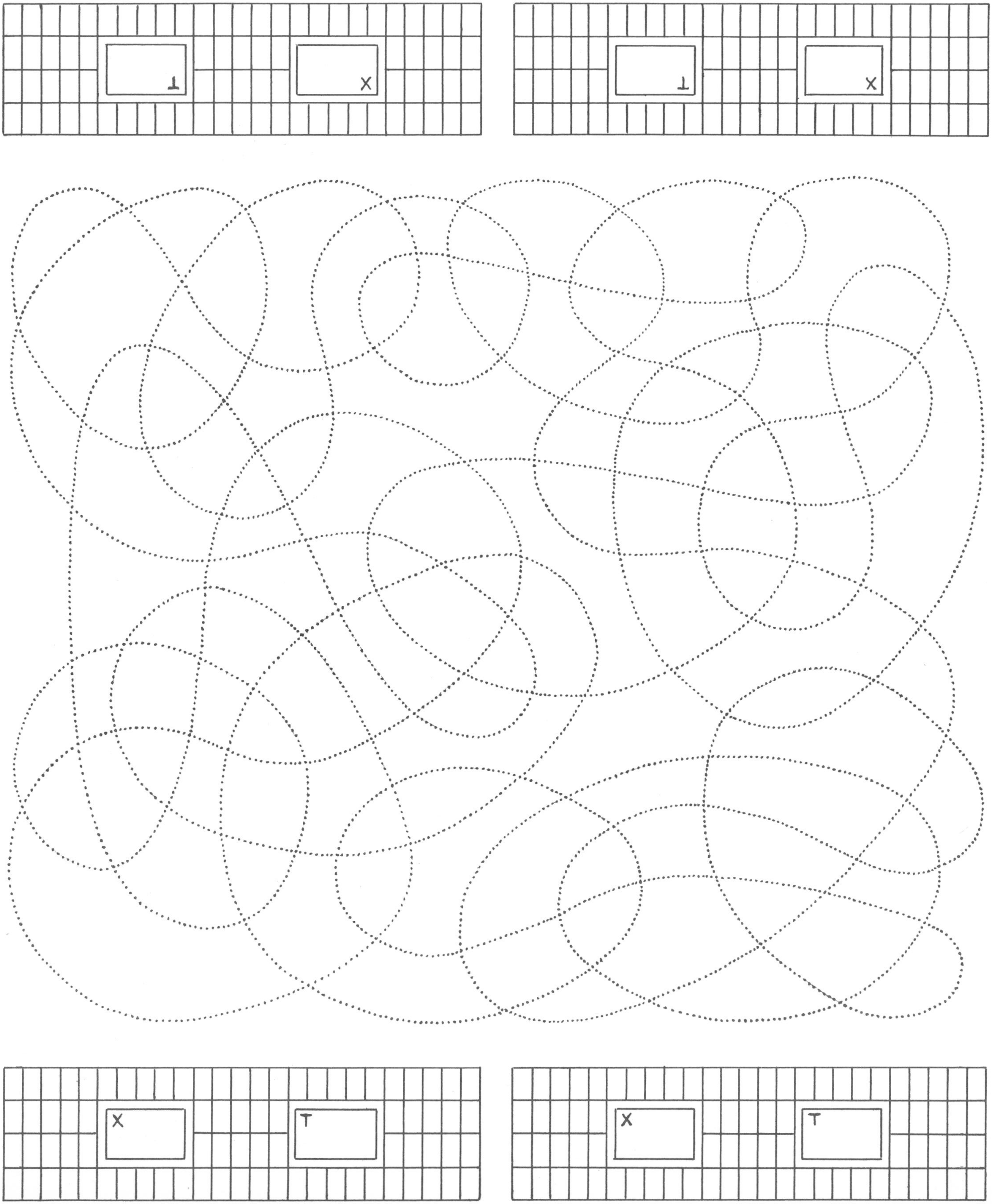

MIRO

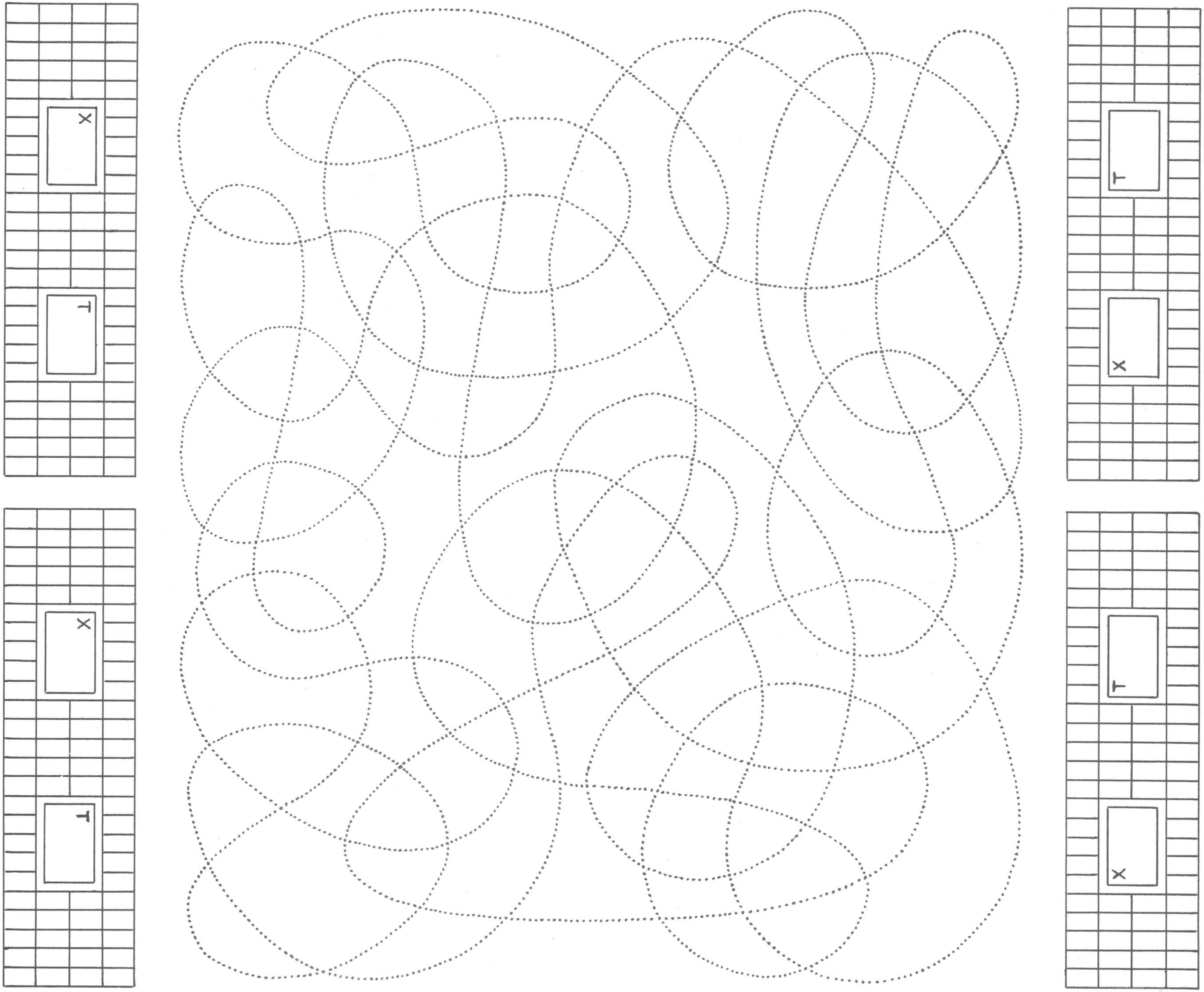

MIRO

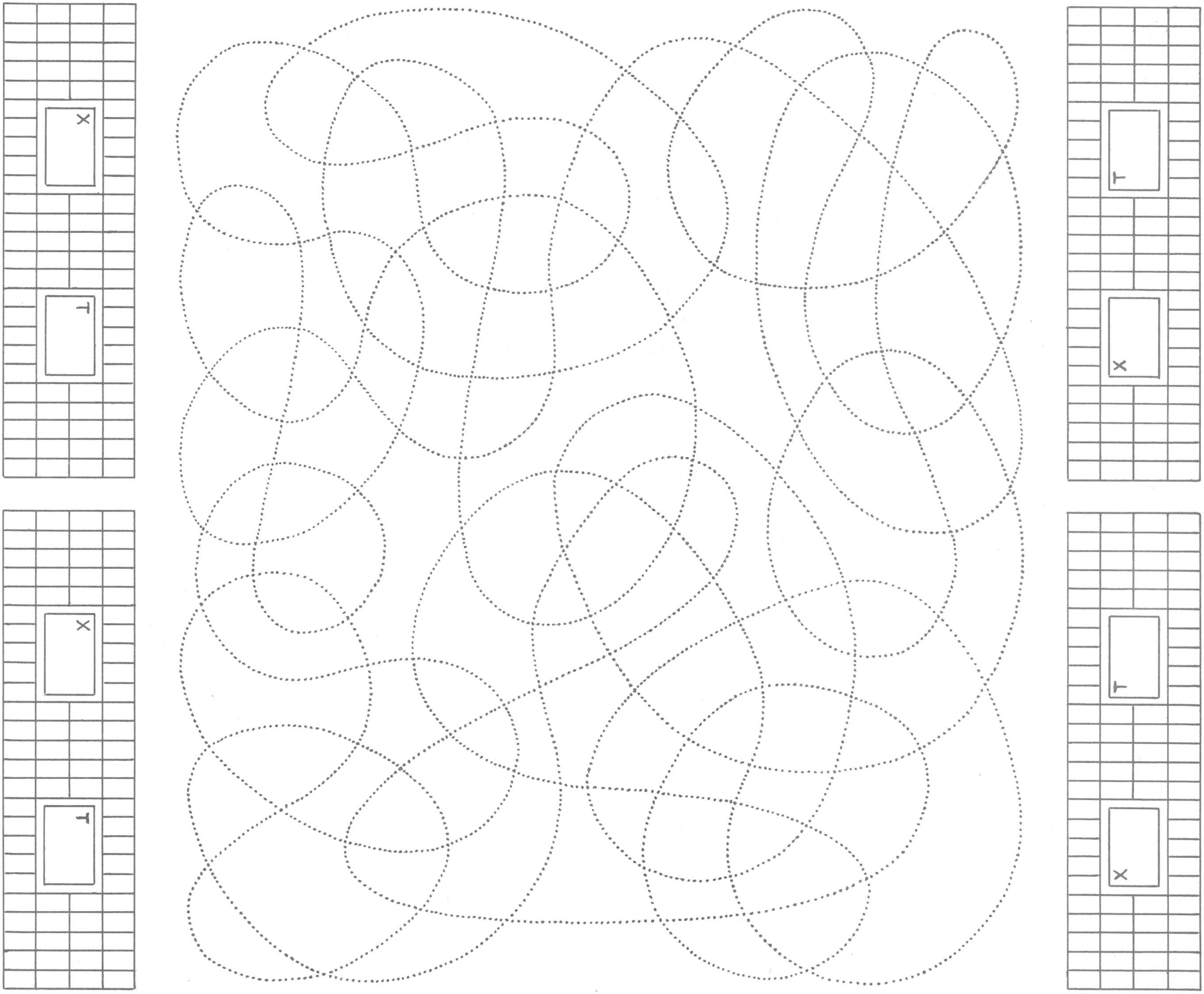

MIRO

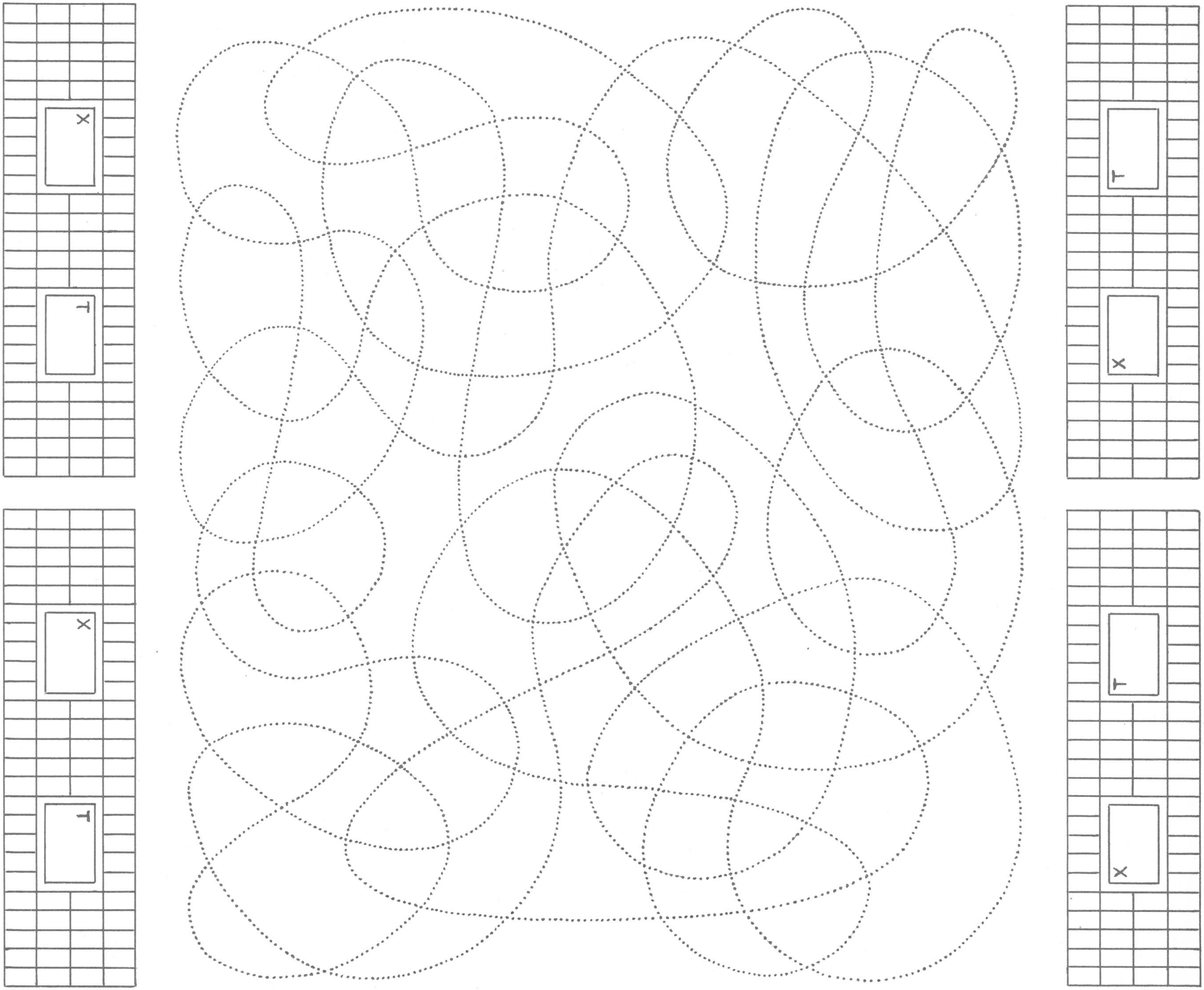

MIRO

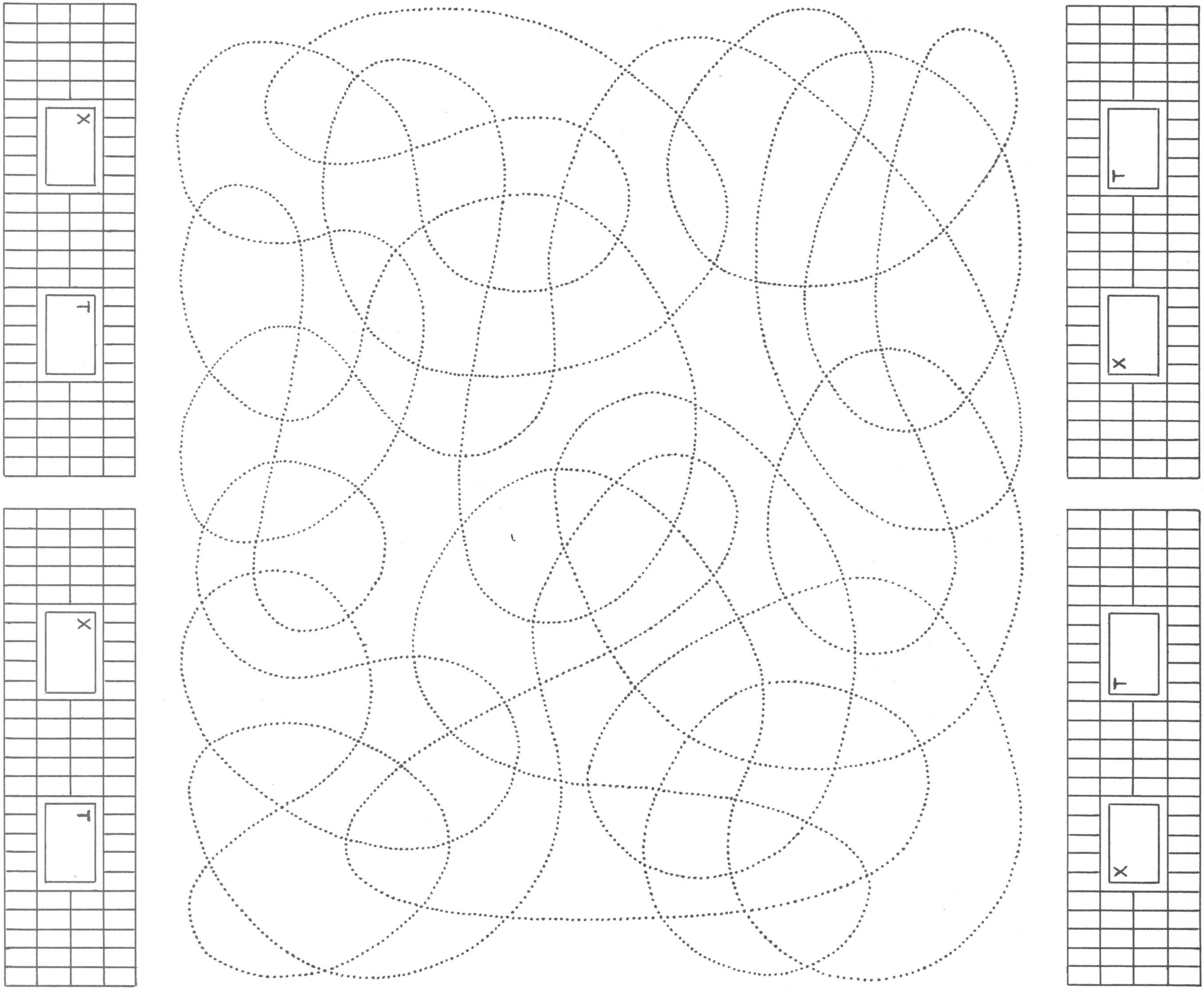

MIRO

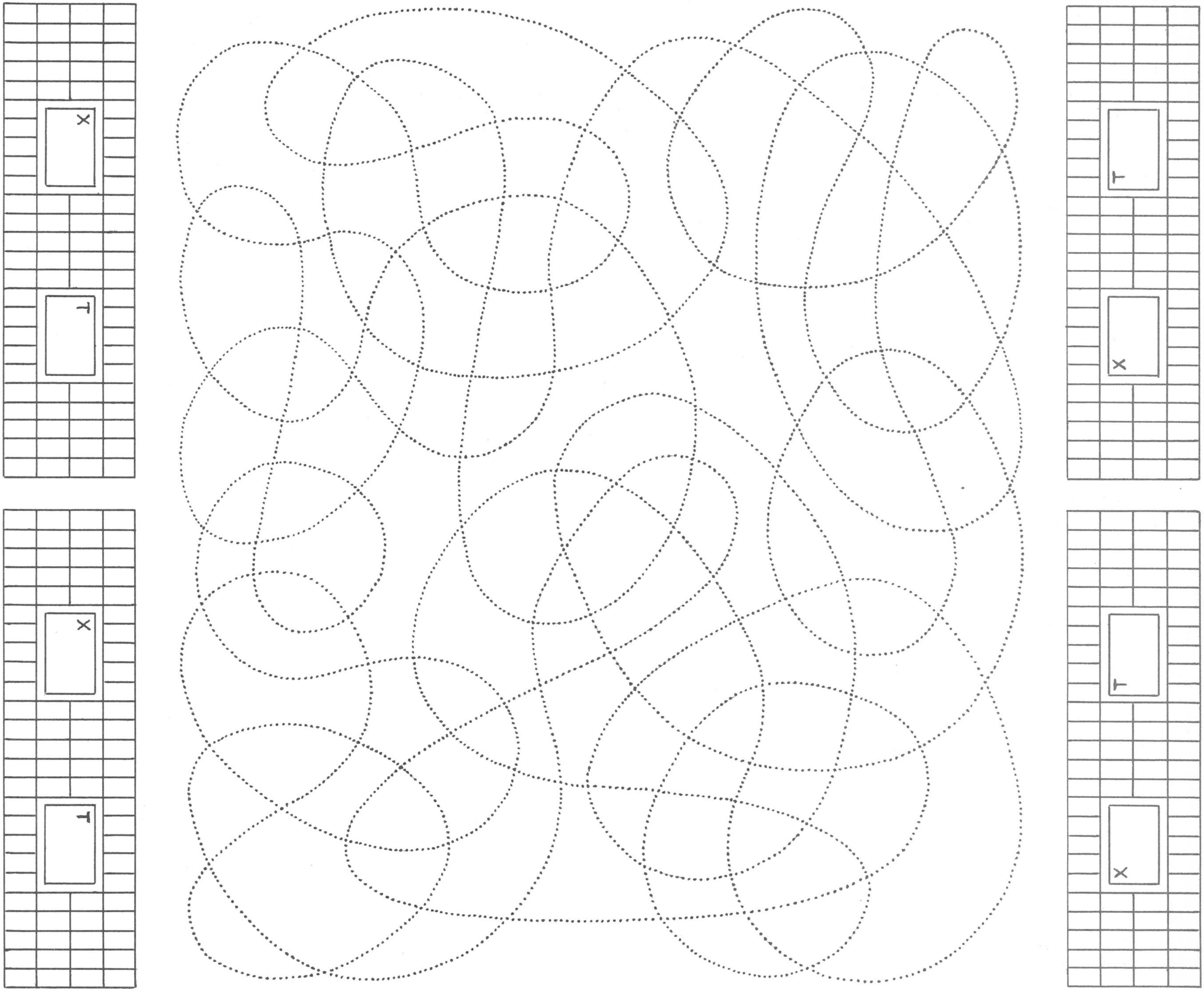

MONDRIAN

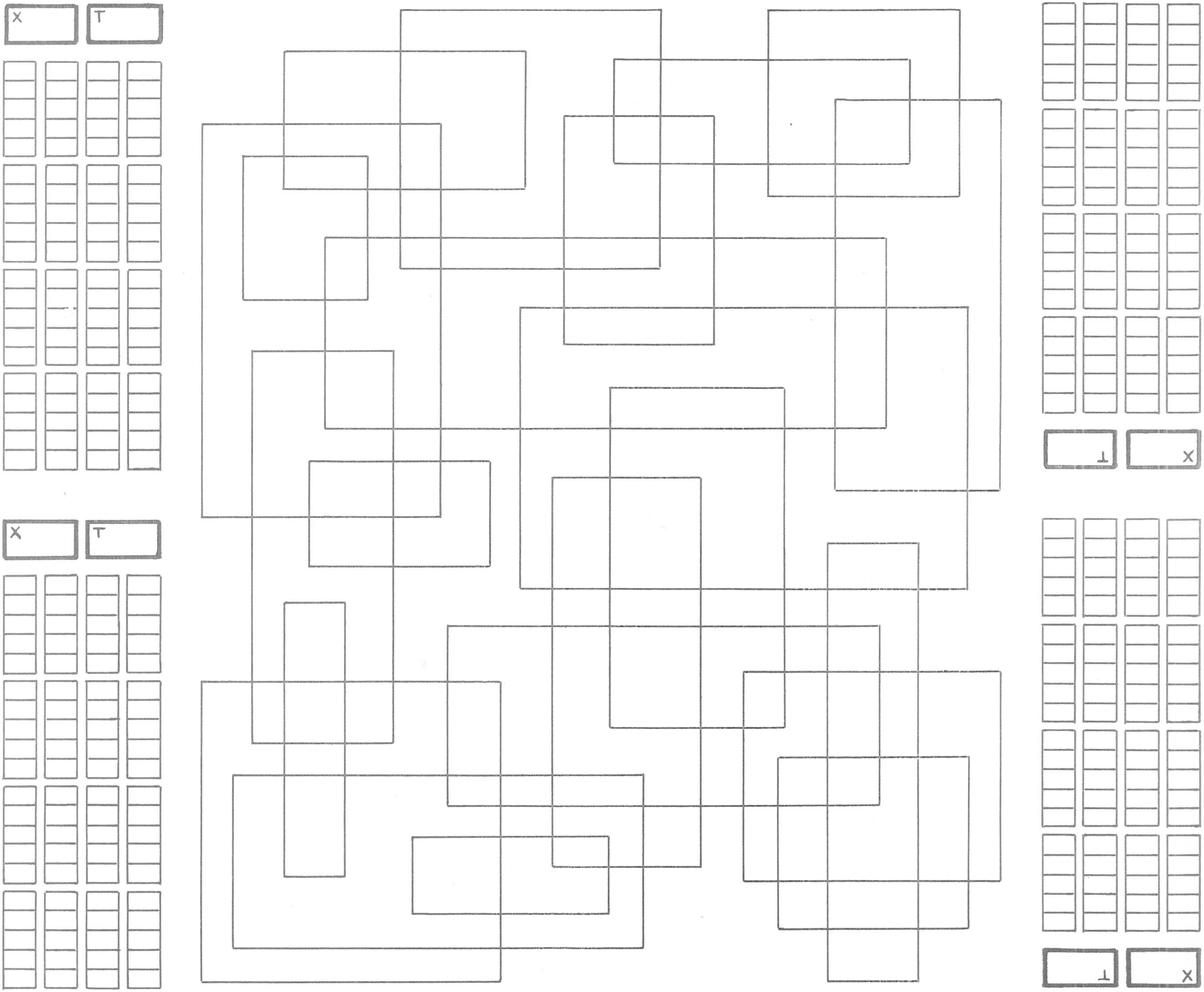

X | T

X | T

T | X

T | X

MONDRIAN

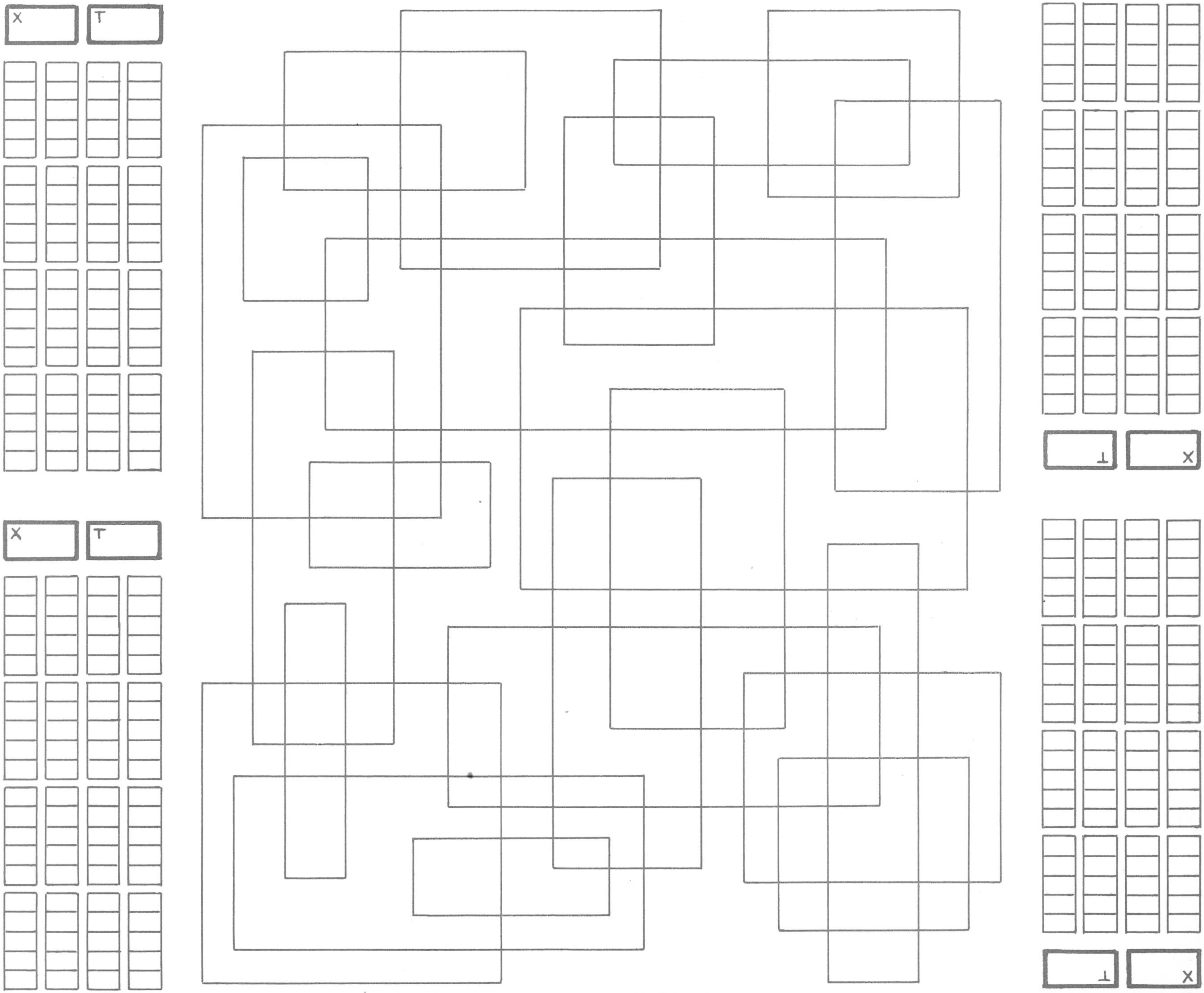

X T

X T

T X

T X

X | T

X | T

T | X

T | X

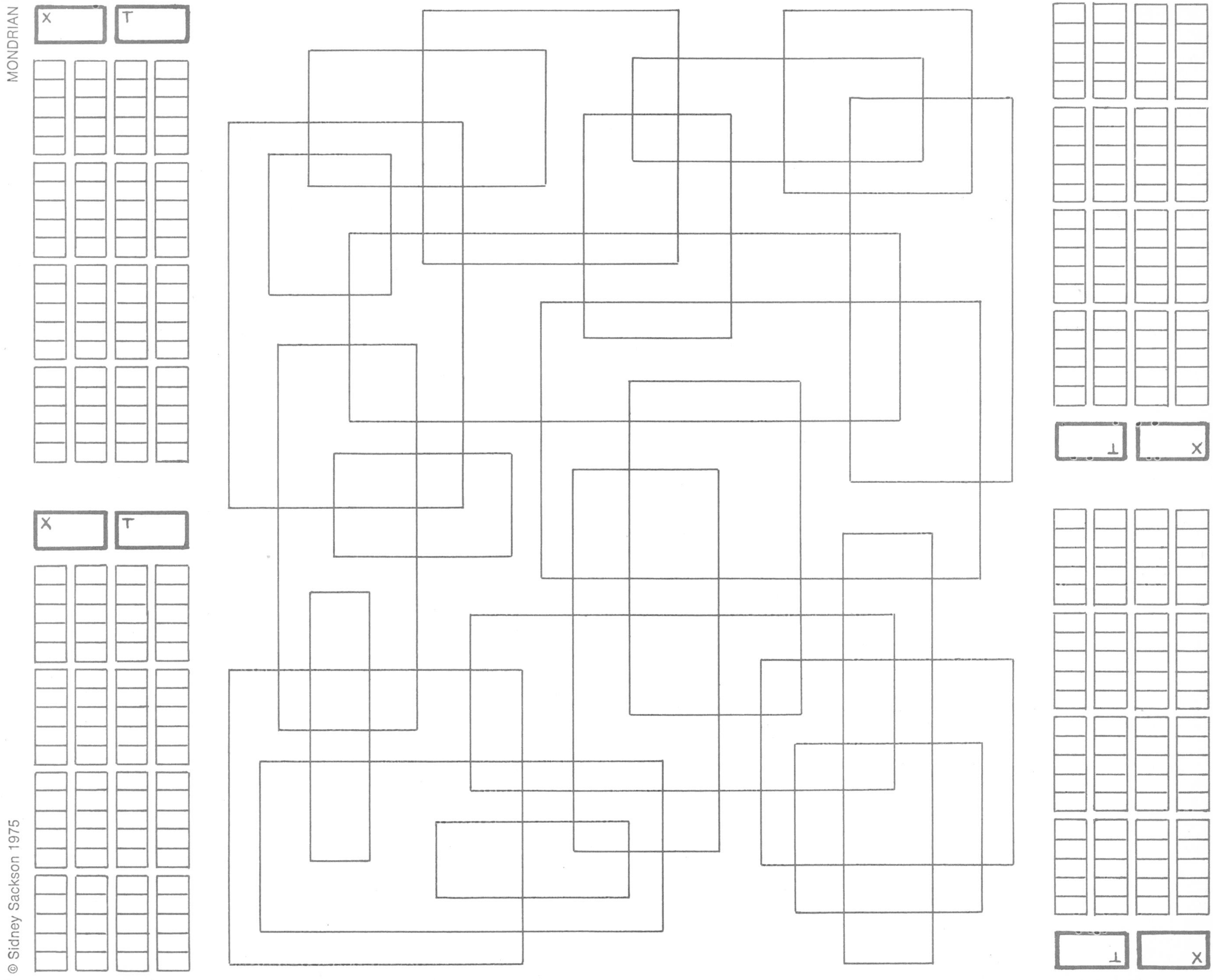
MONDRIAN
X
T
© Sidney Sackson 1975

X T

X T

⊥ X

⊥ X

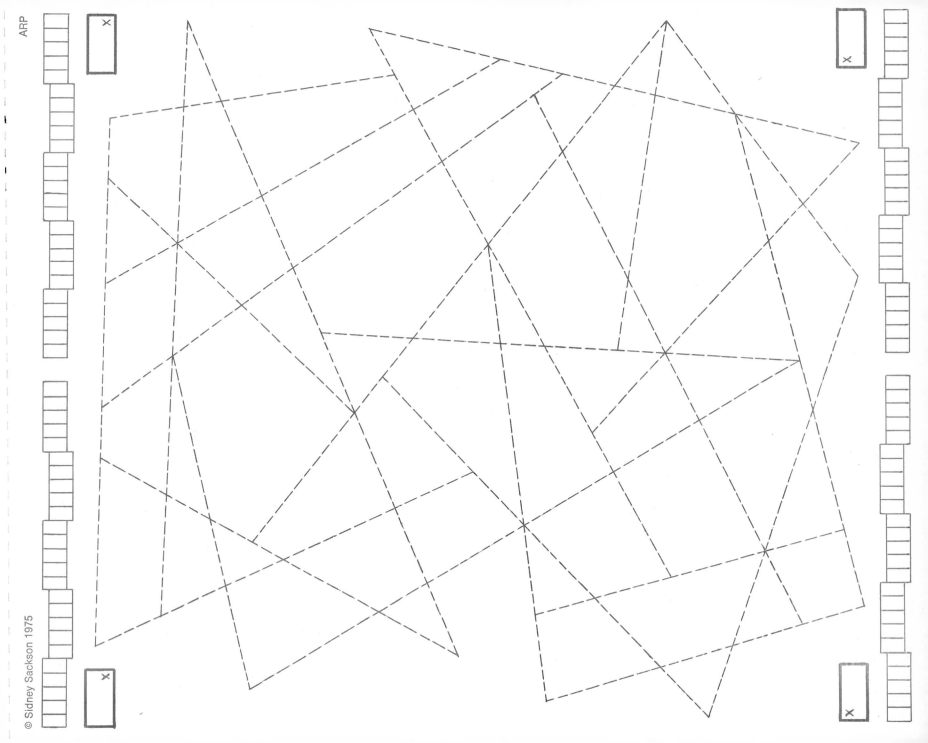

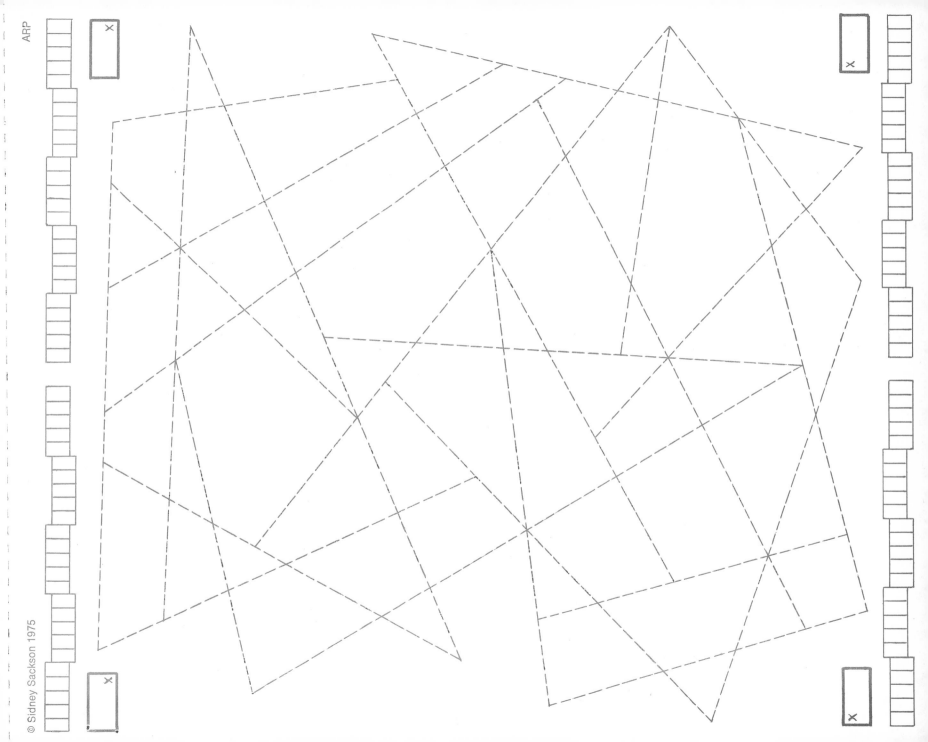

ARP

© Sidney Sackson 1975

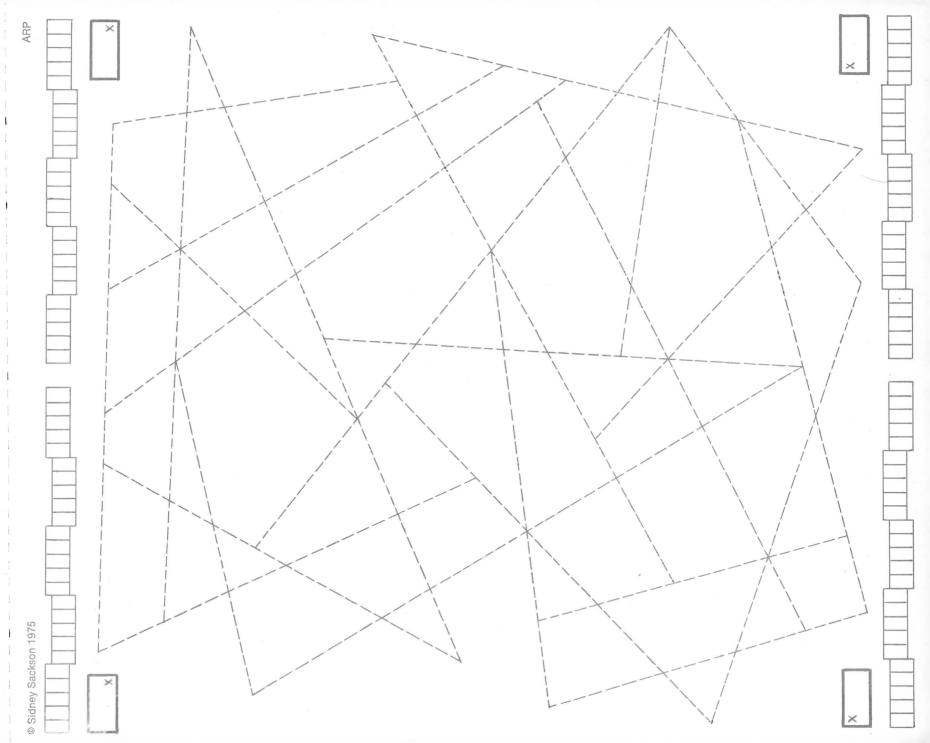

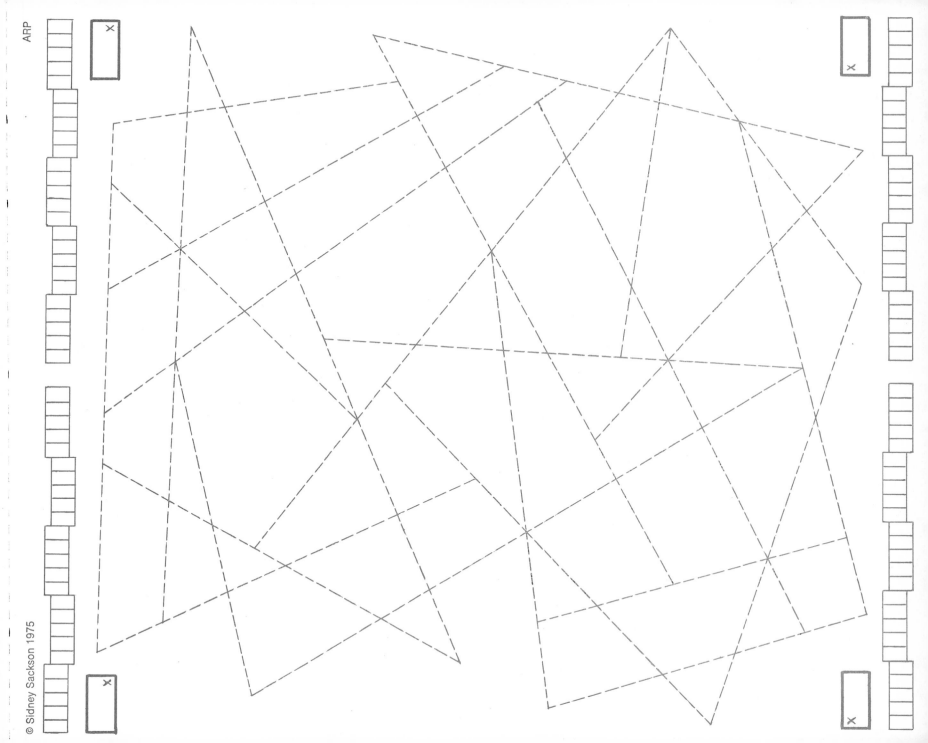

ARP

© Sidney Sackson 1975

ARP

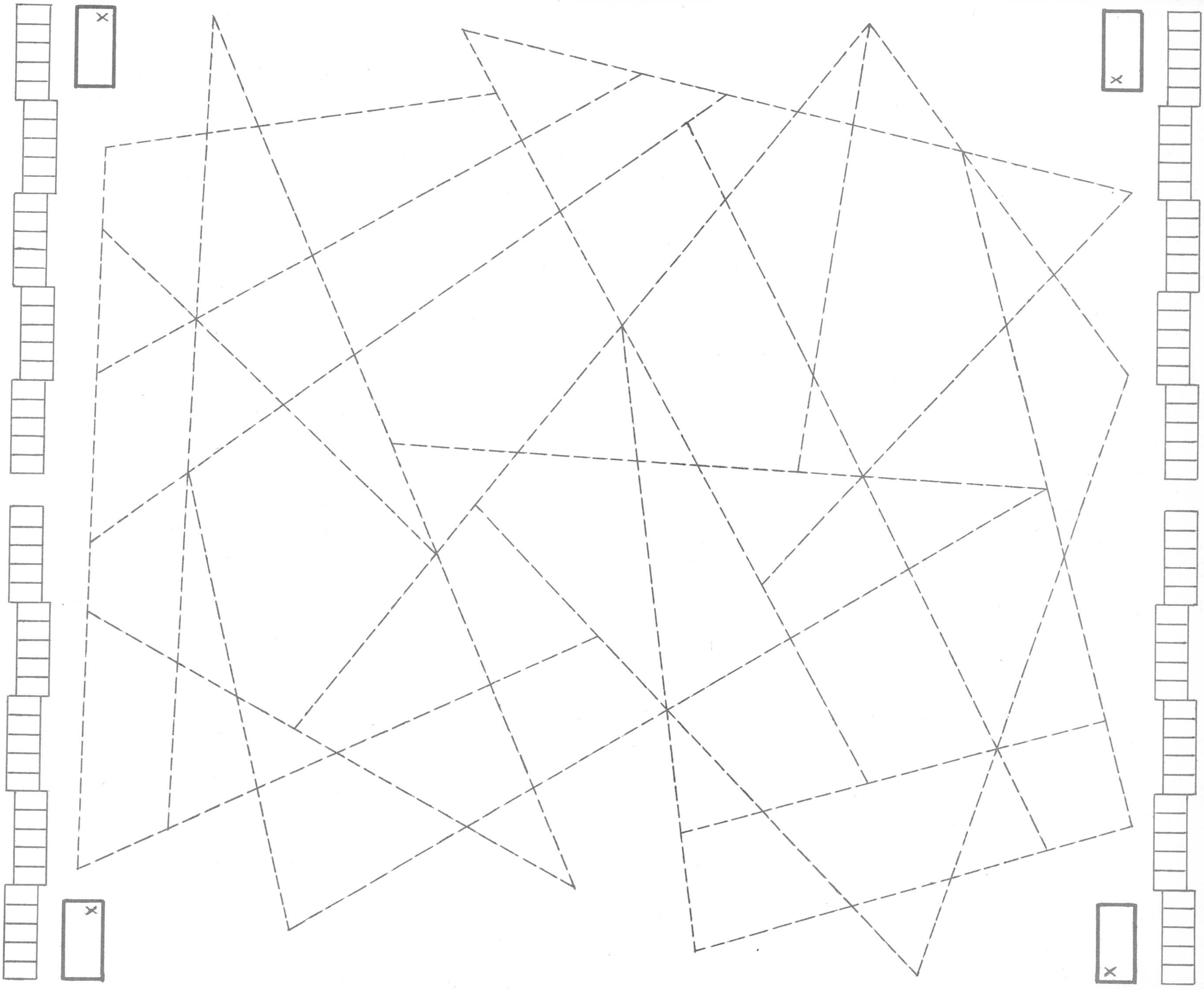

ARP

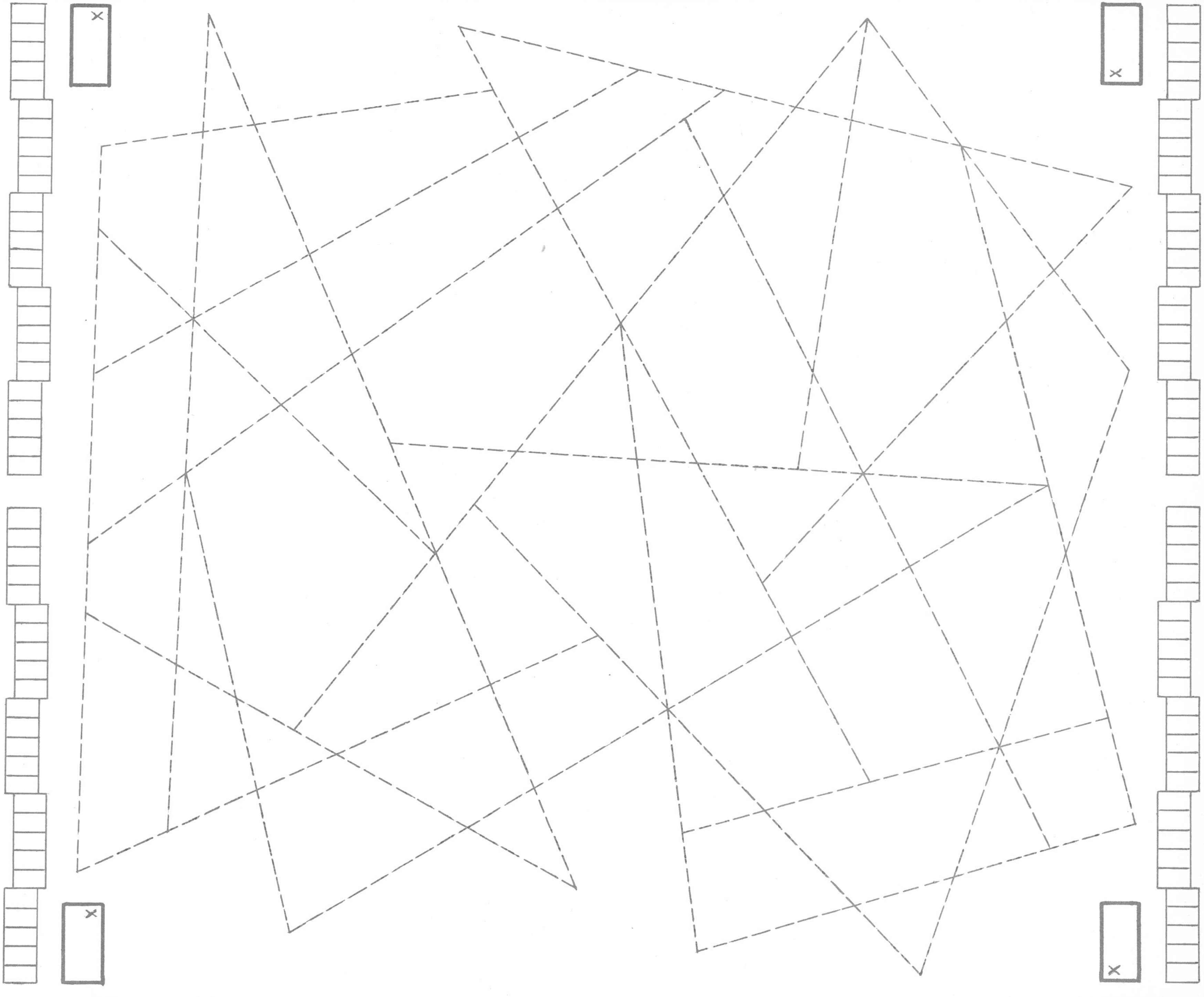

ARP

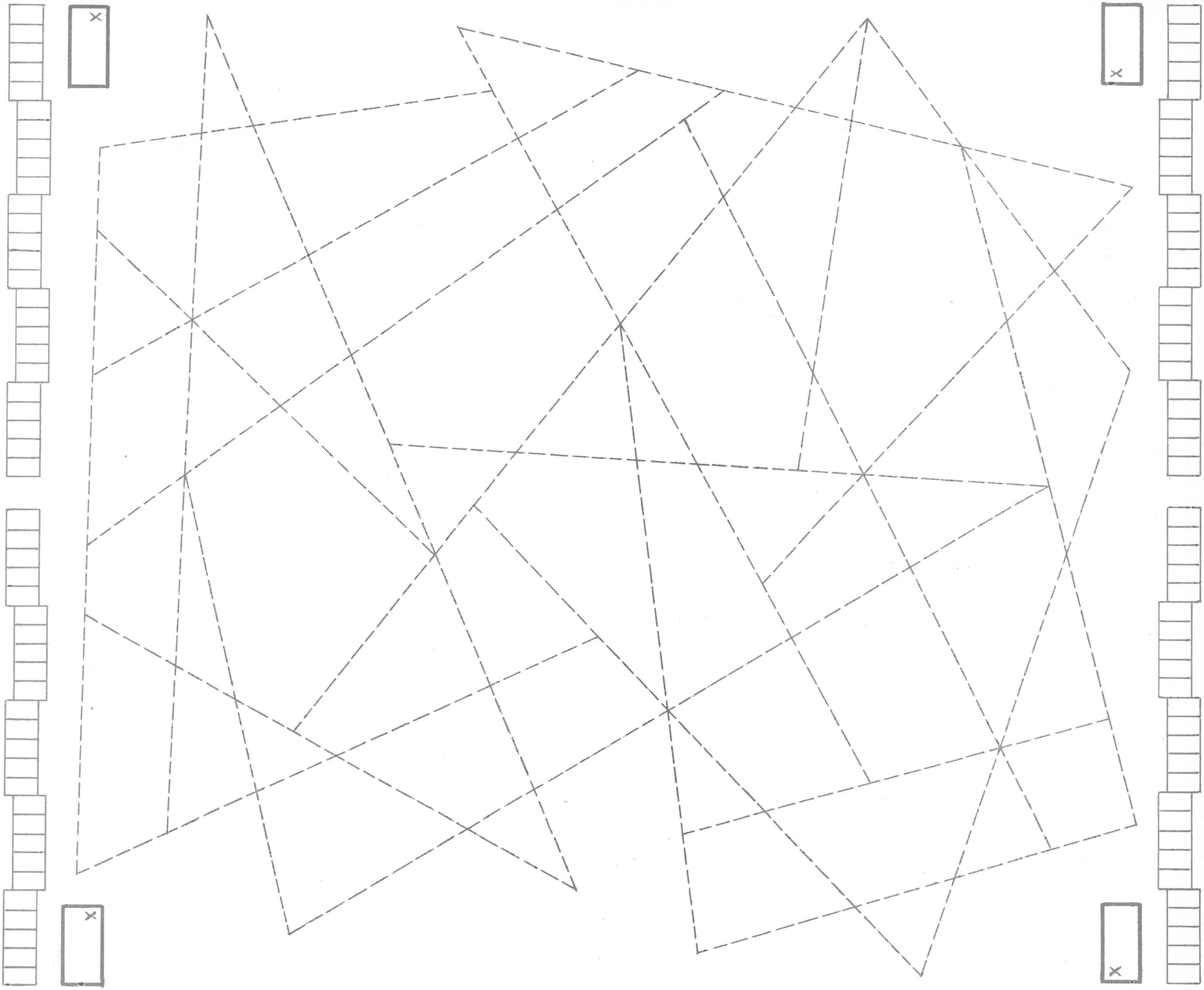

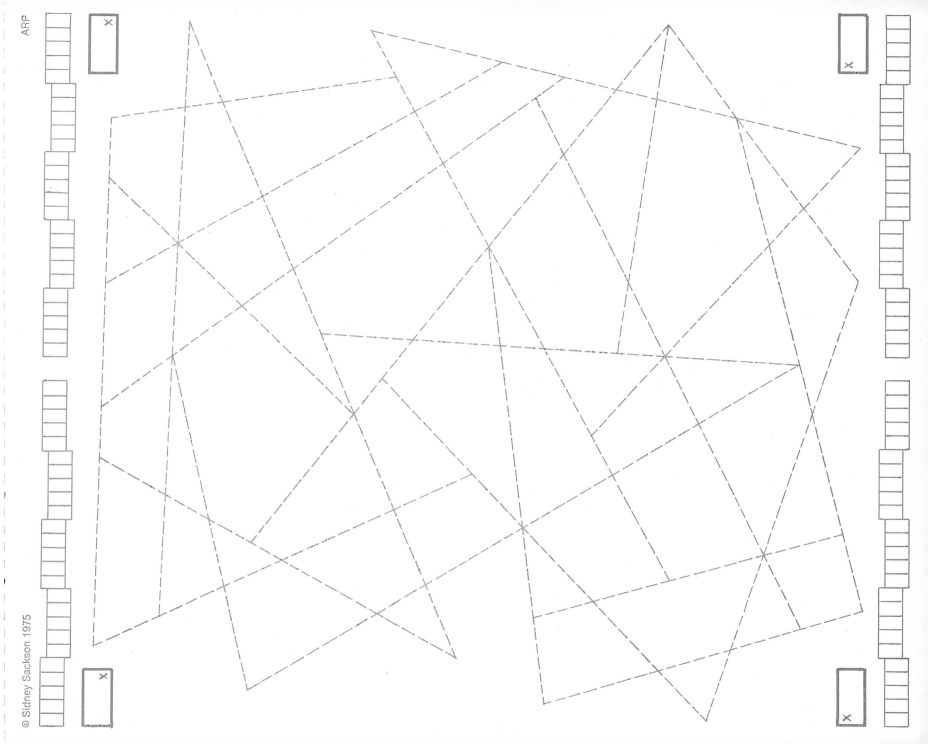

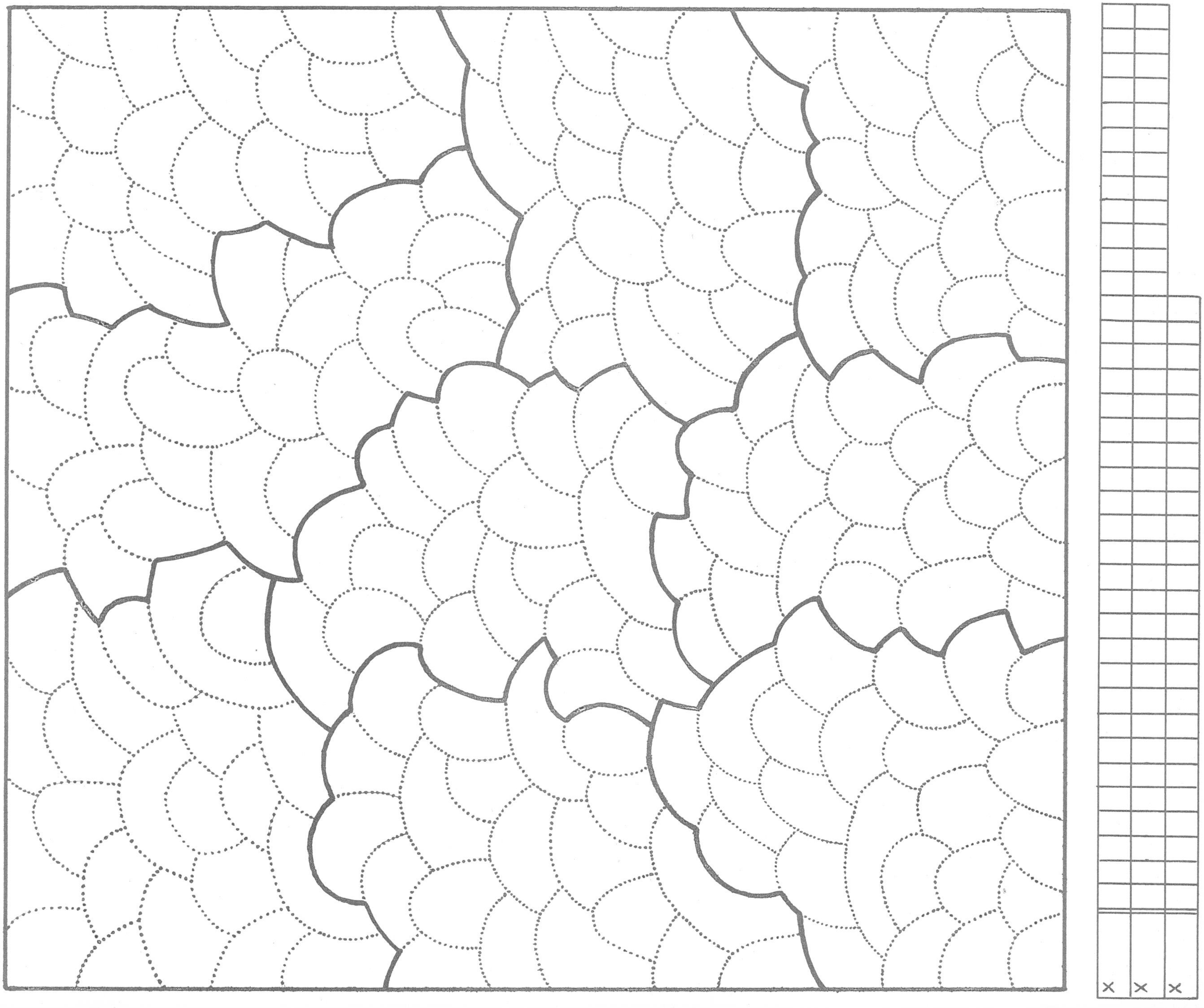

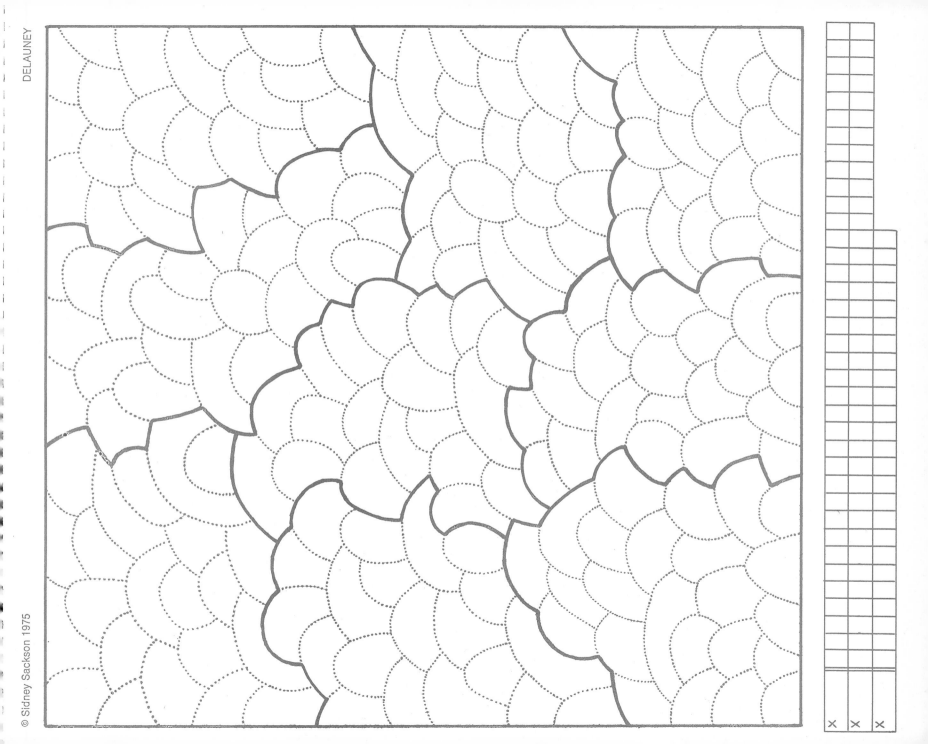

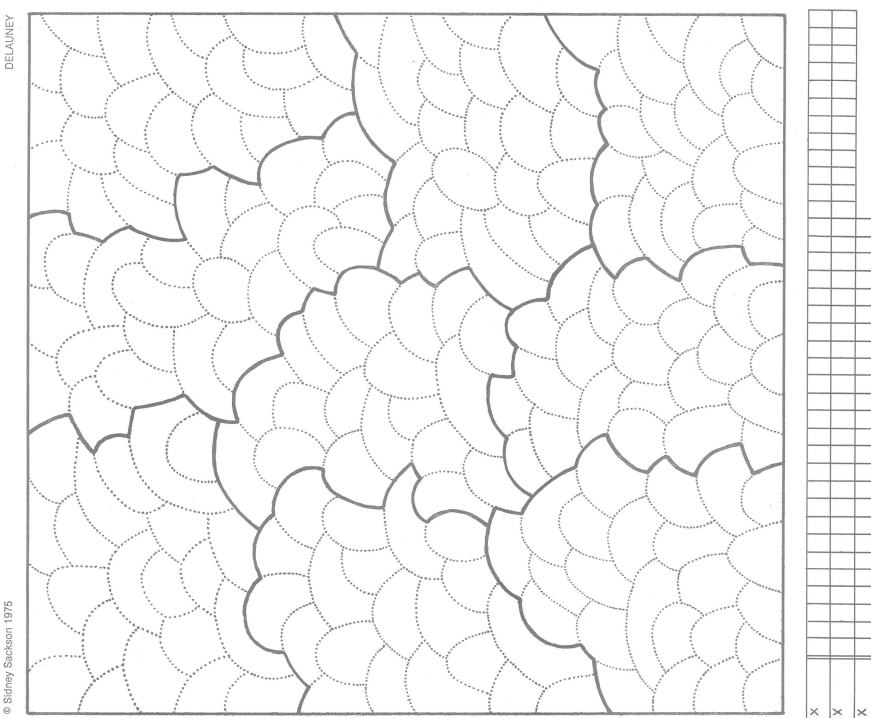

DELAUNEY

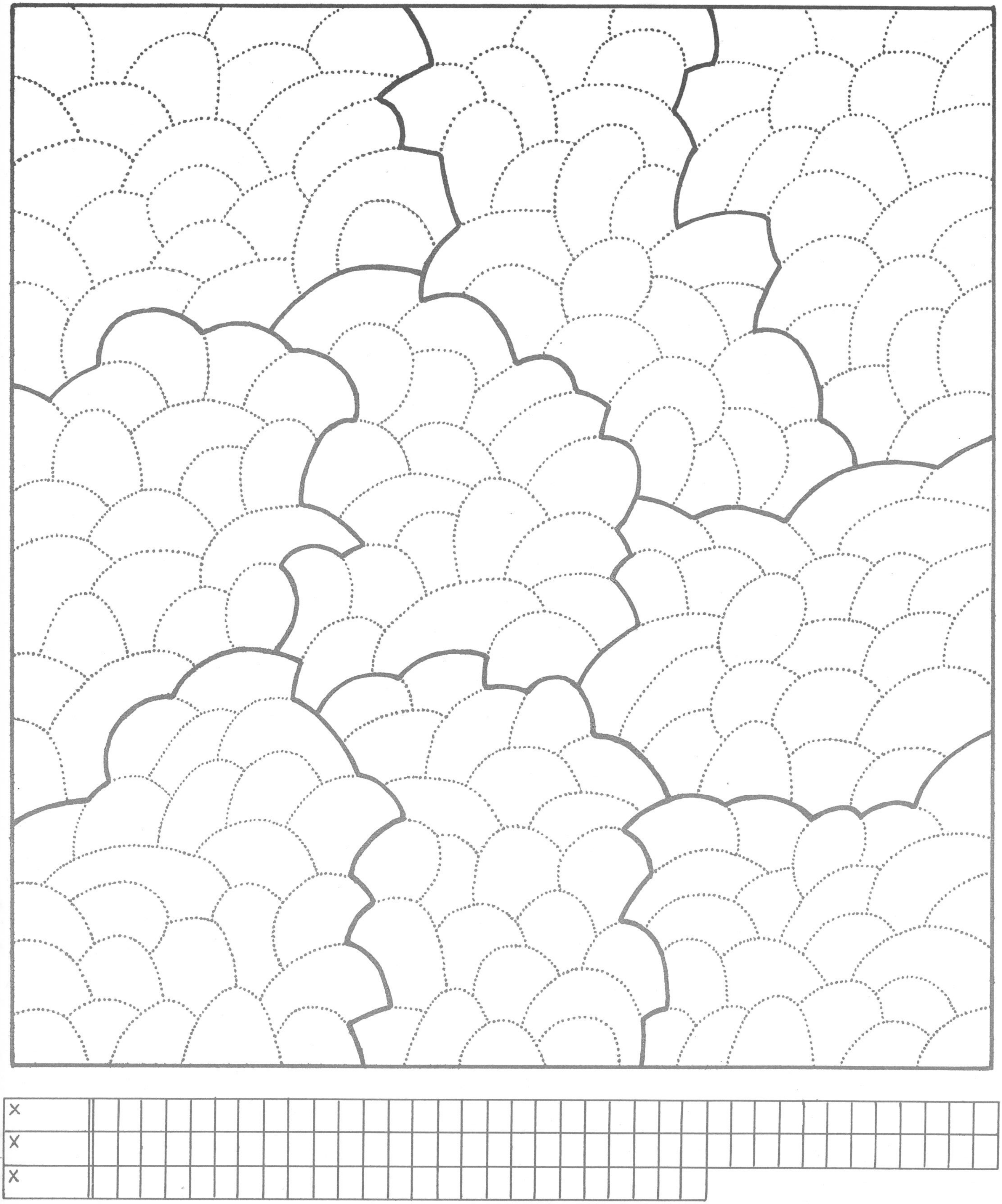

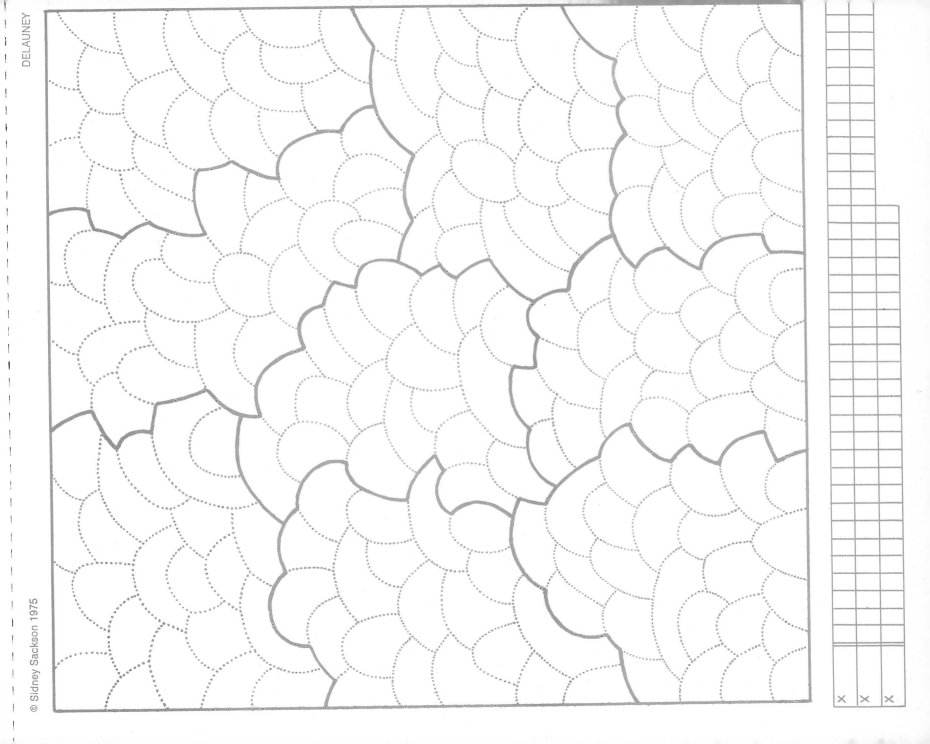

DELAUNEY

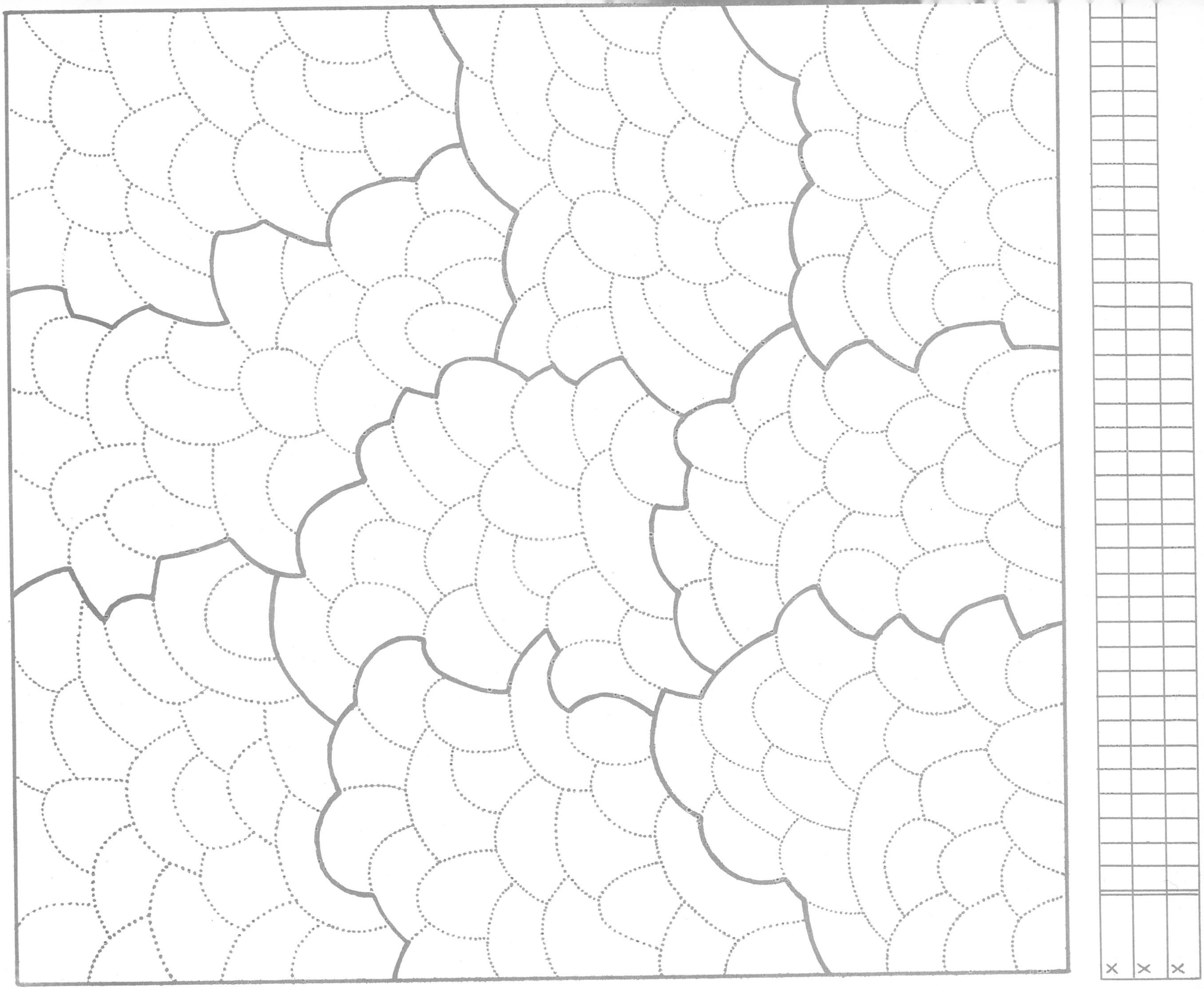

| × | × | × |

KLEE

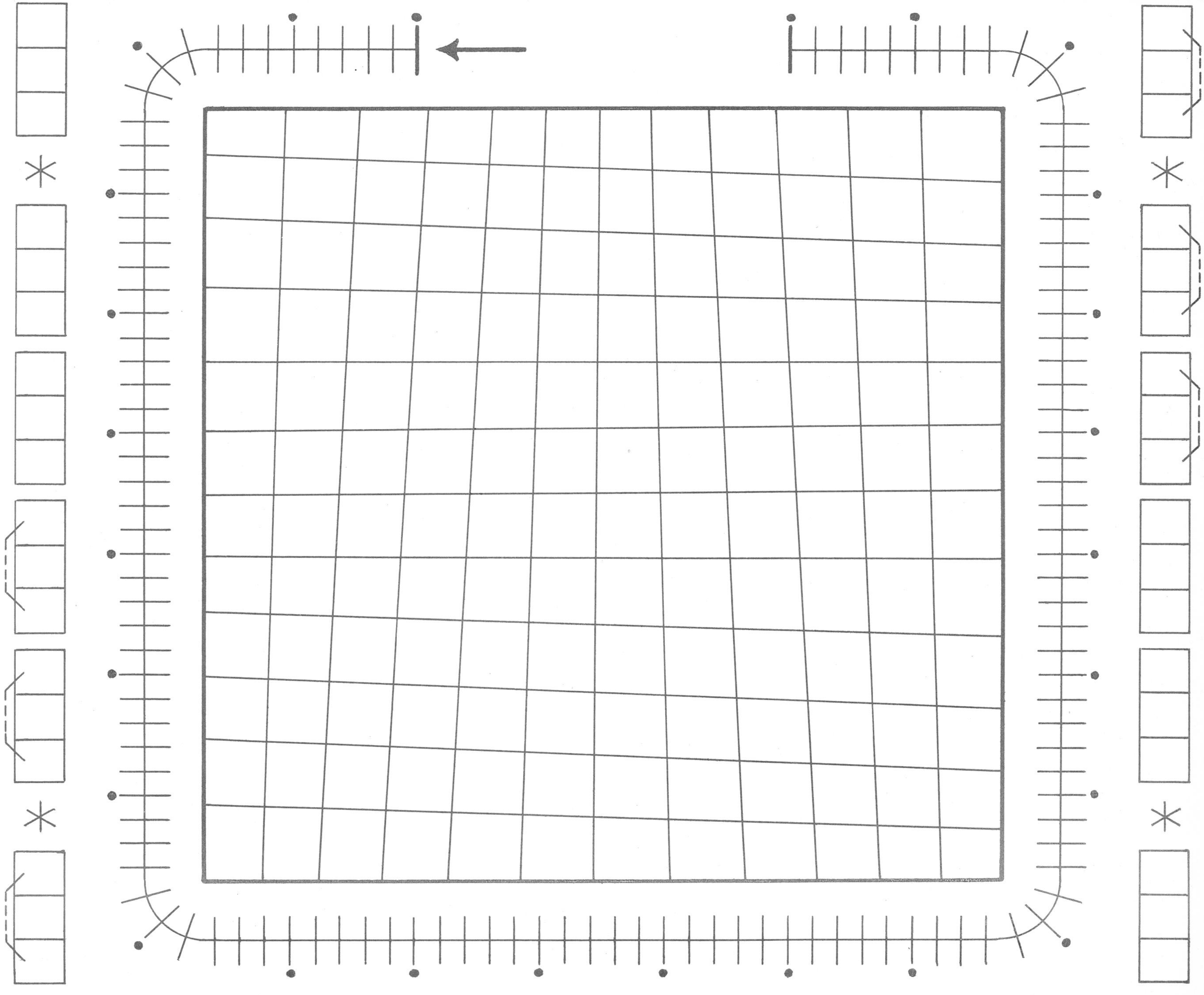

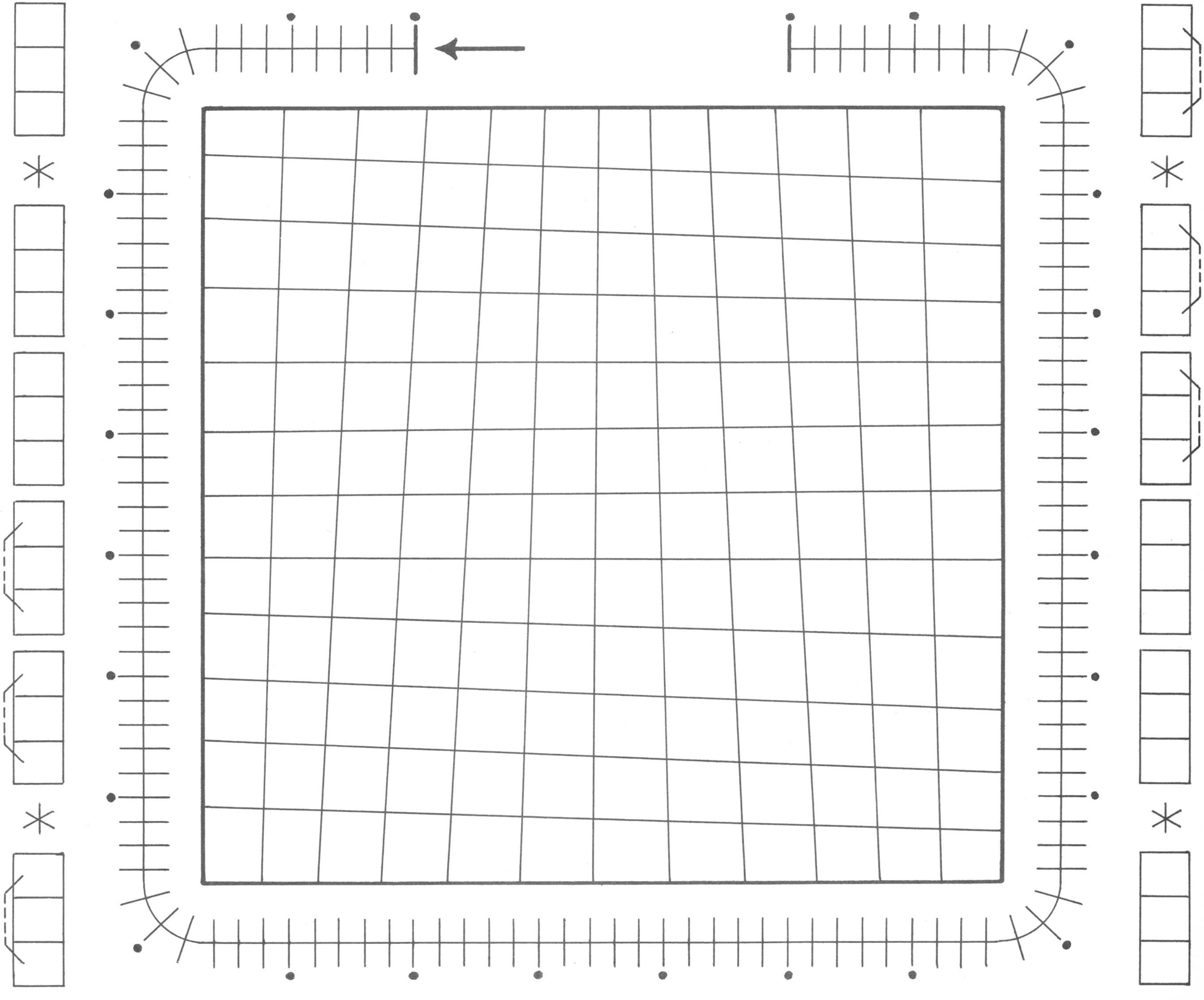
KLEE

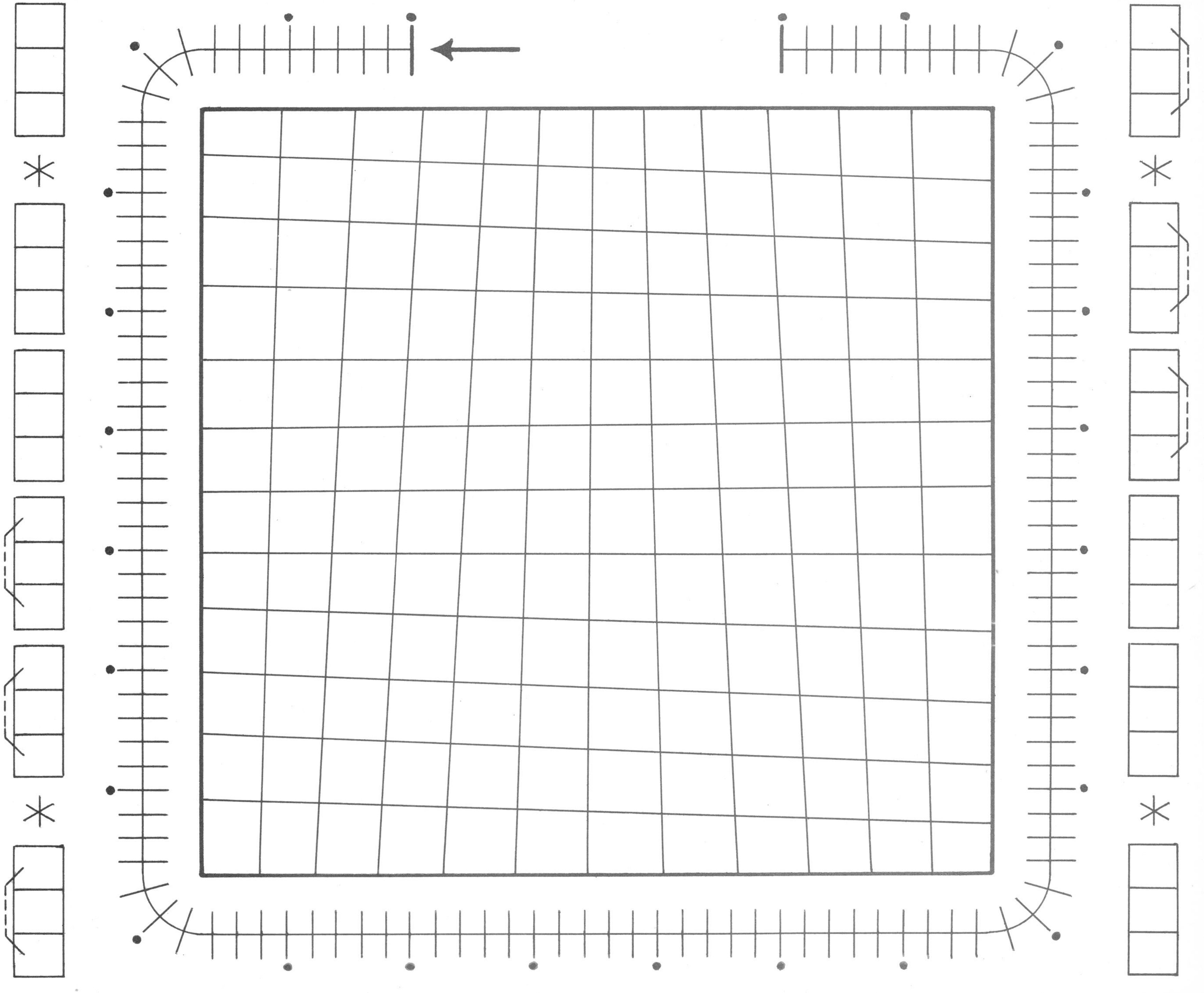
KLEE
© Sidney Sackson 1975

KLEE

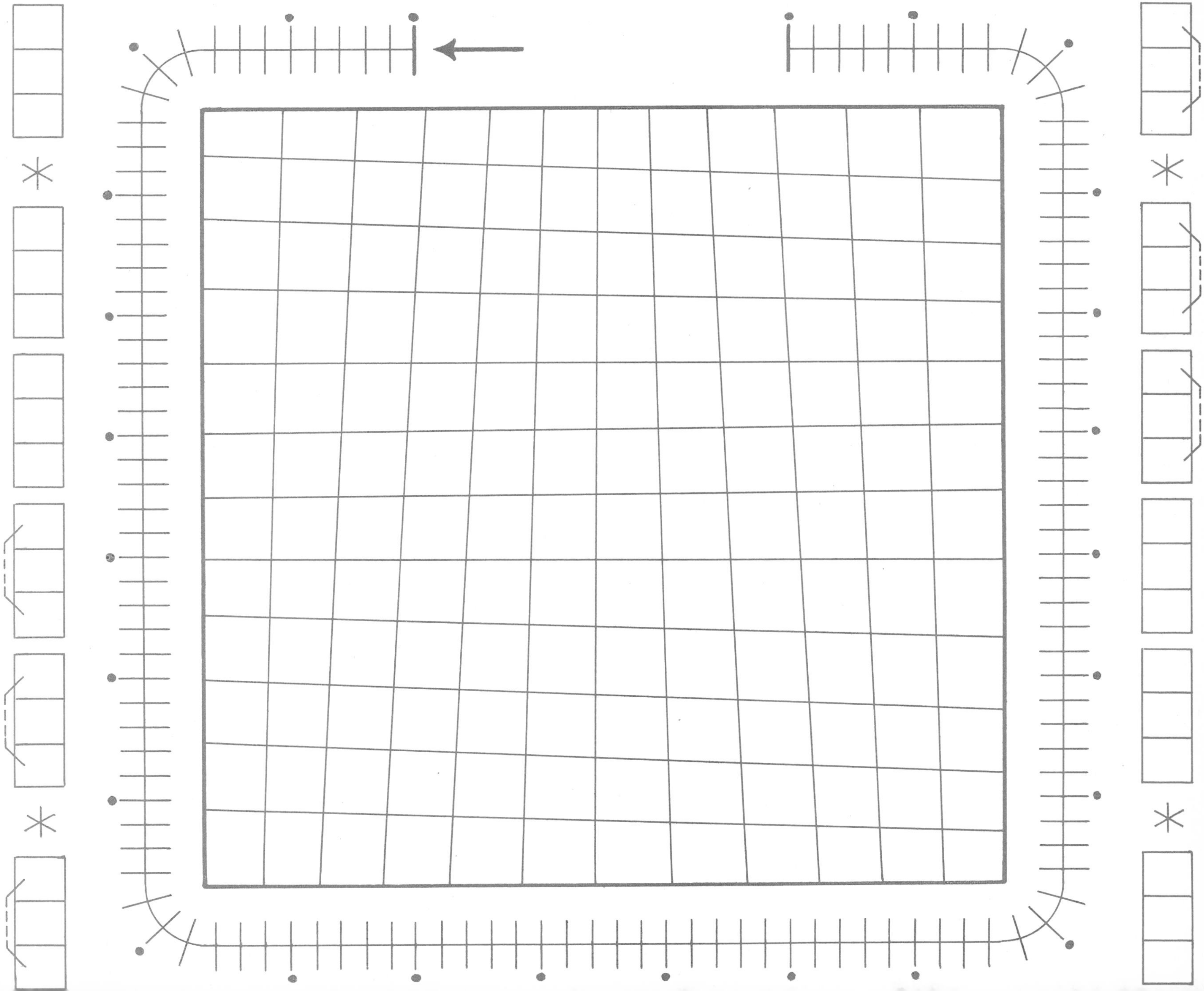

KLEE

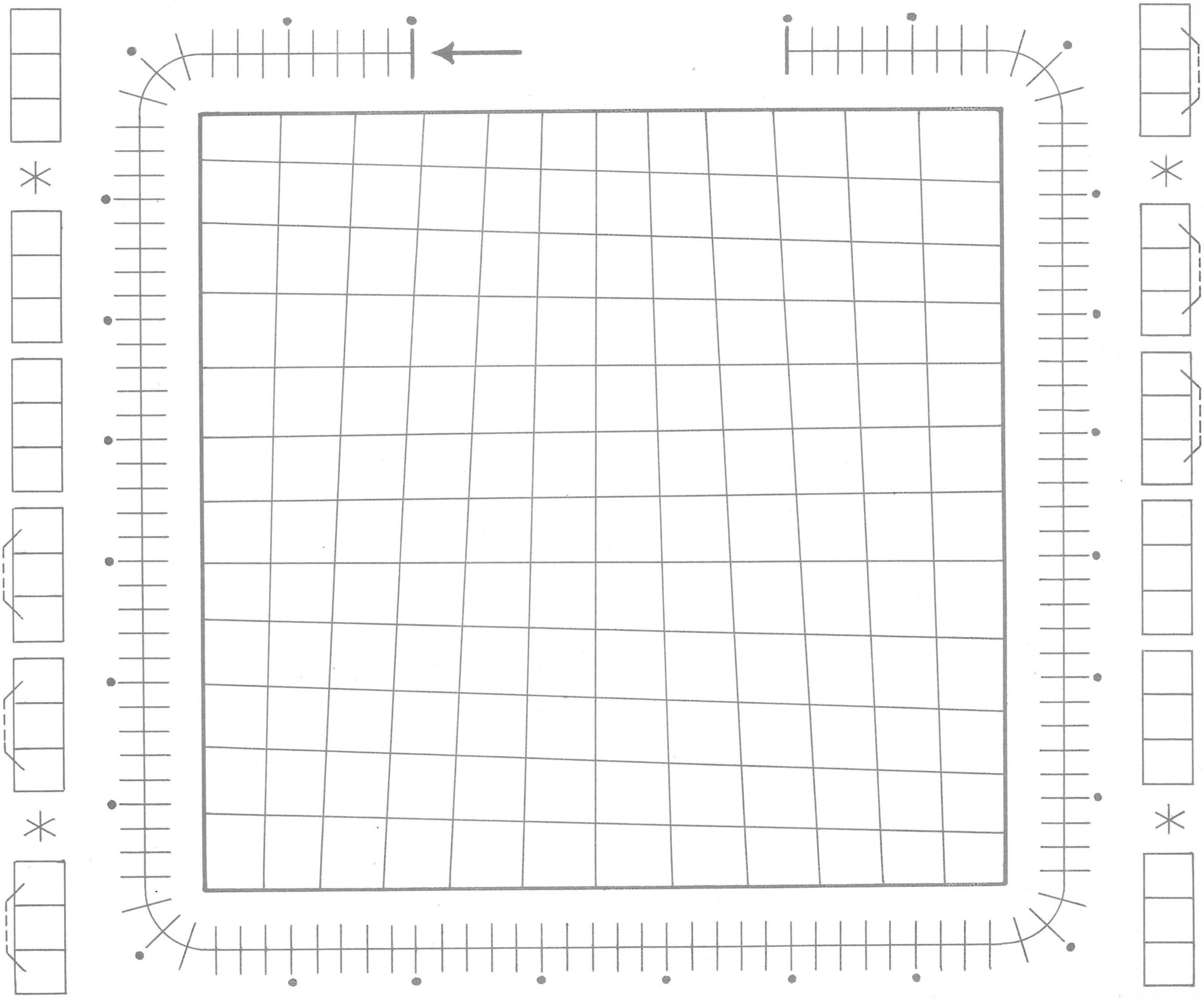

KLEE

© Sidney Sackson 1975

SPRINGER

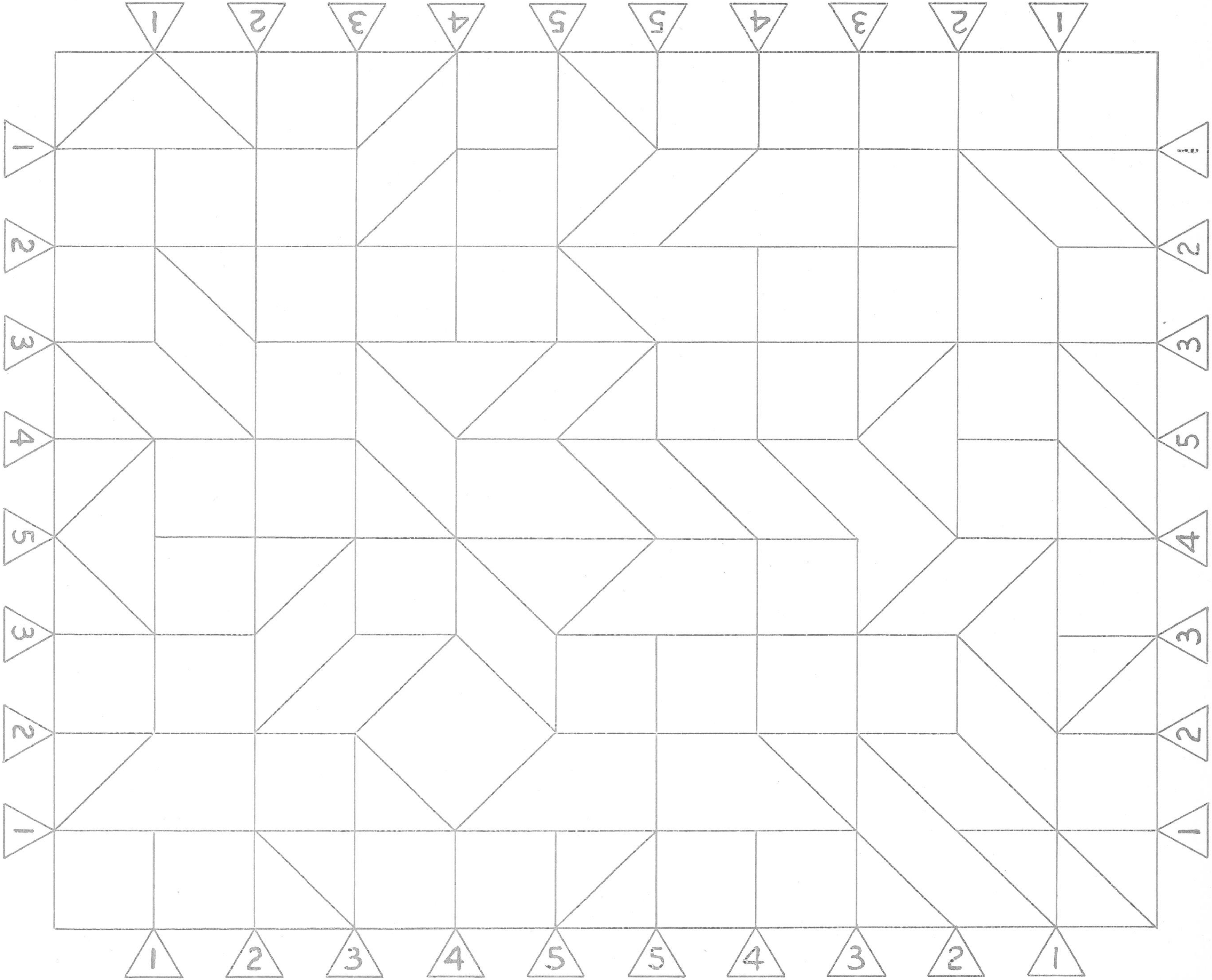

SPRINGER

SPRINGER

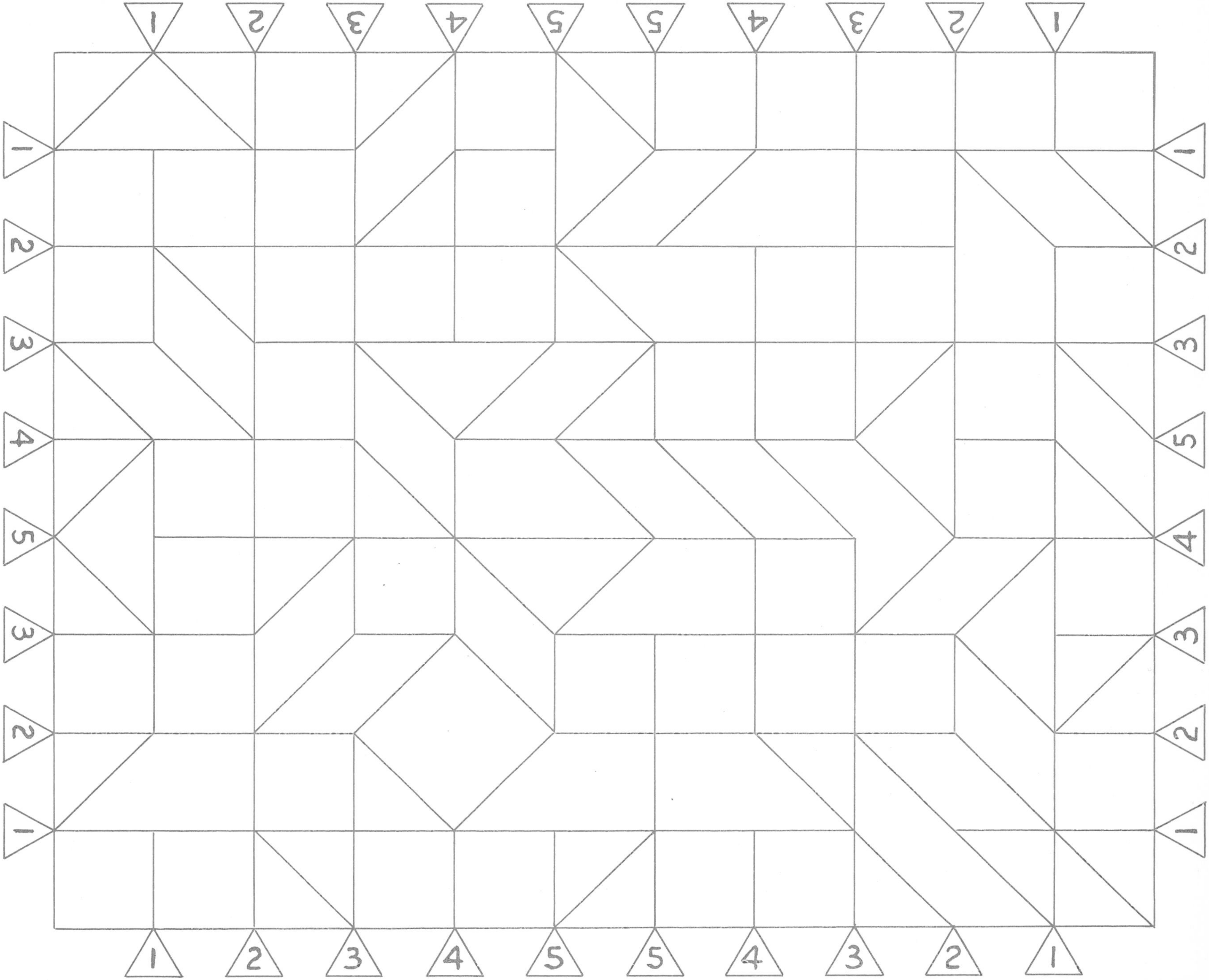

SPRINGER

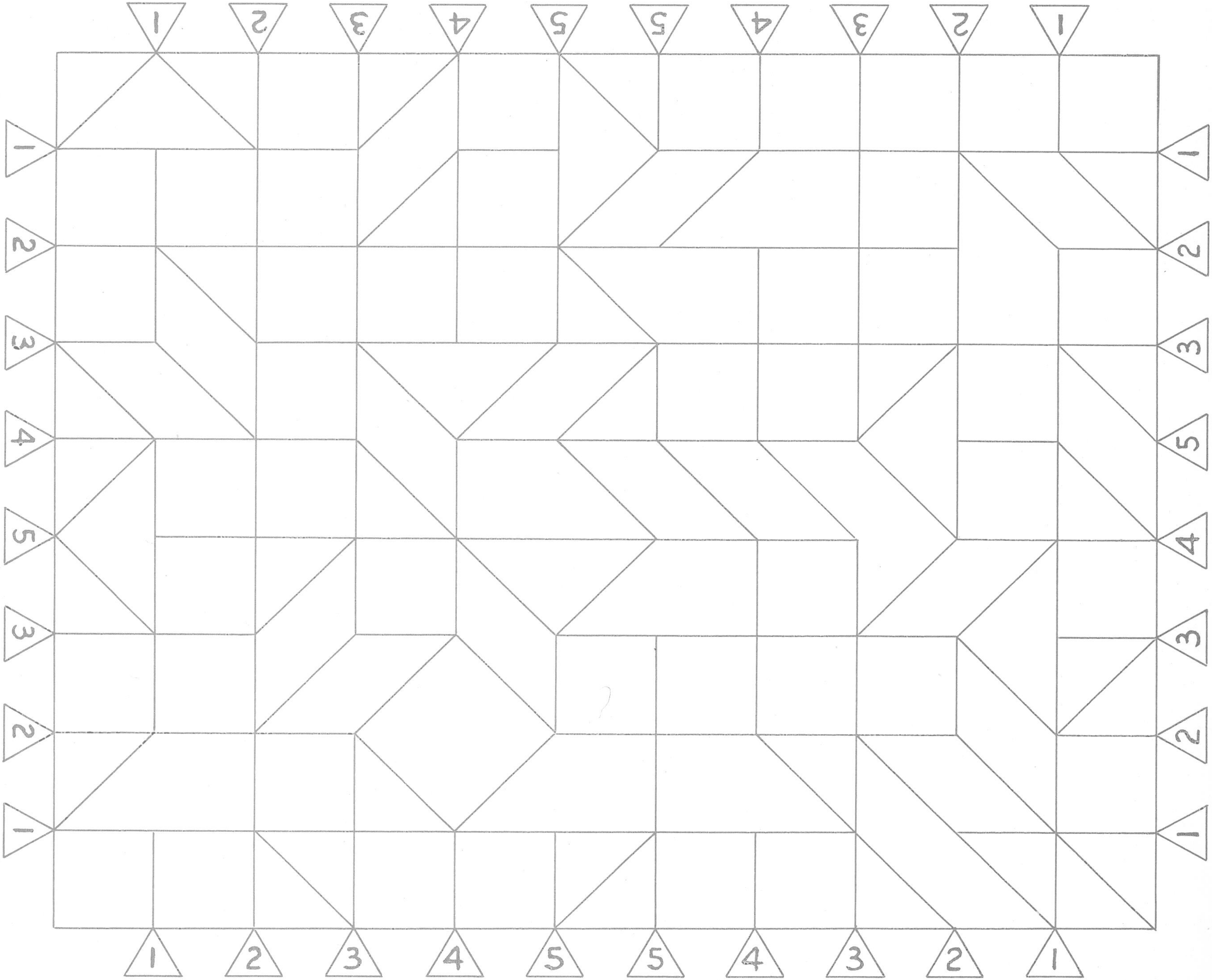

SPRINGER

SPRINGER

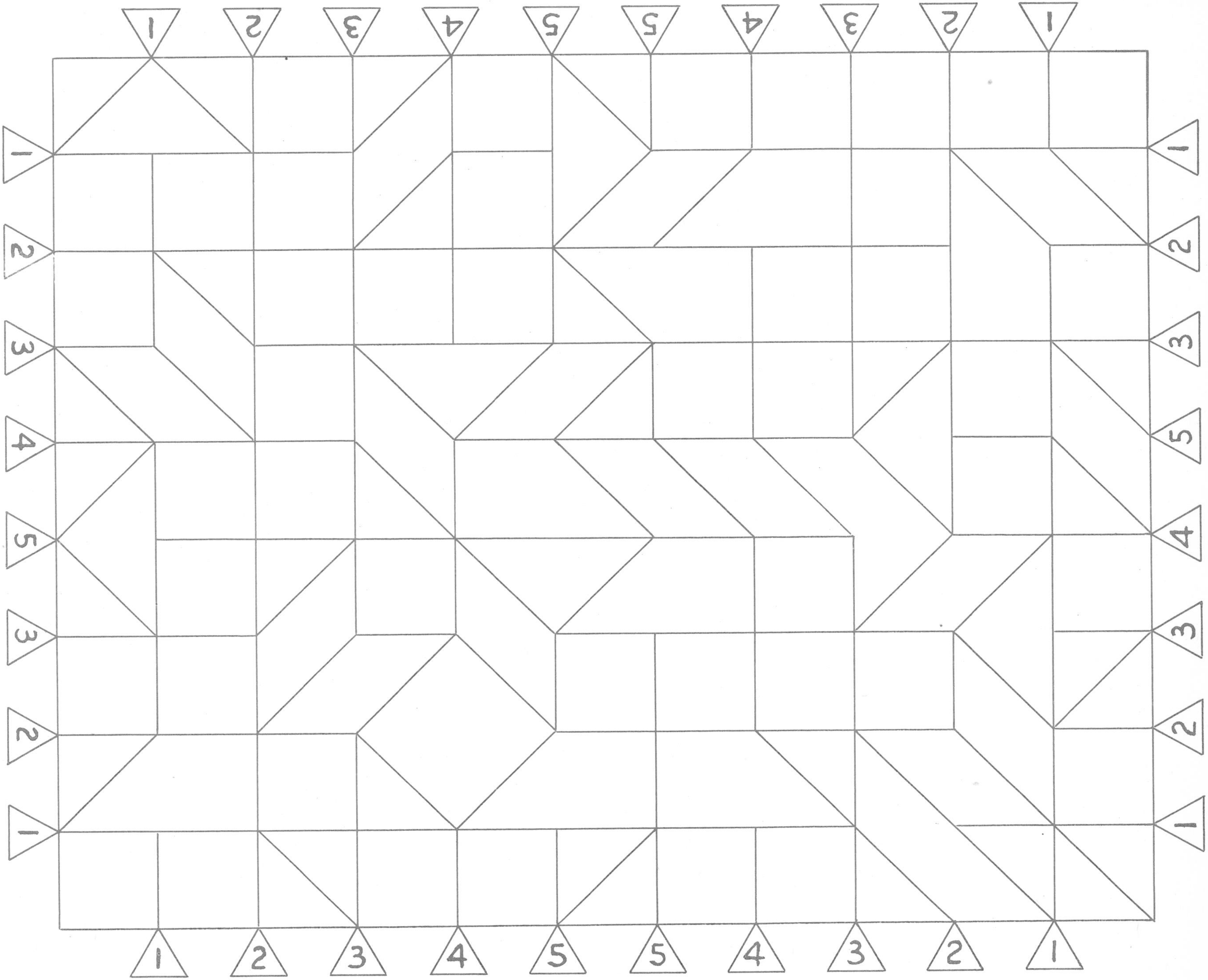

SPRINGER

© Sidney Sackson 1975

SPRINGER

SPRINGER

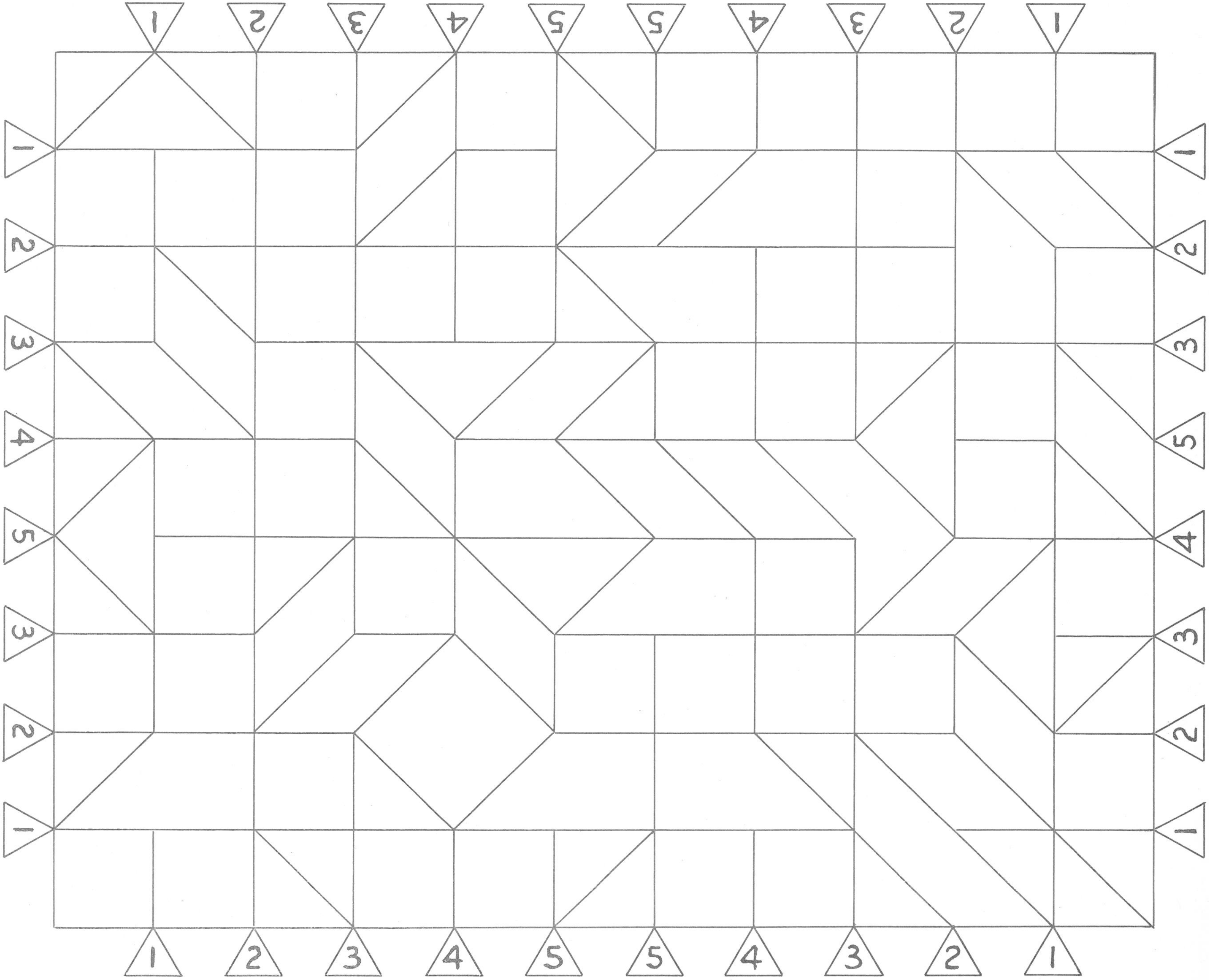

SPRINGER

SPRINGER

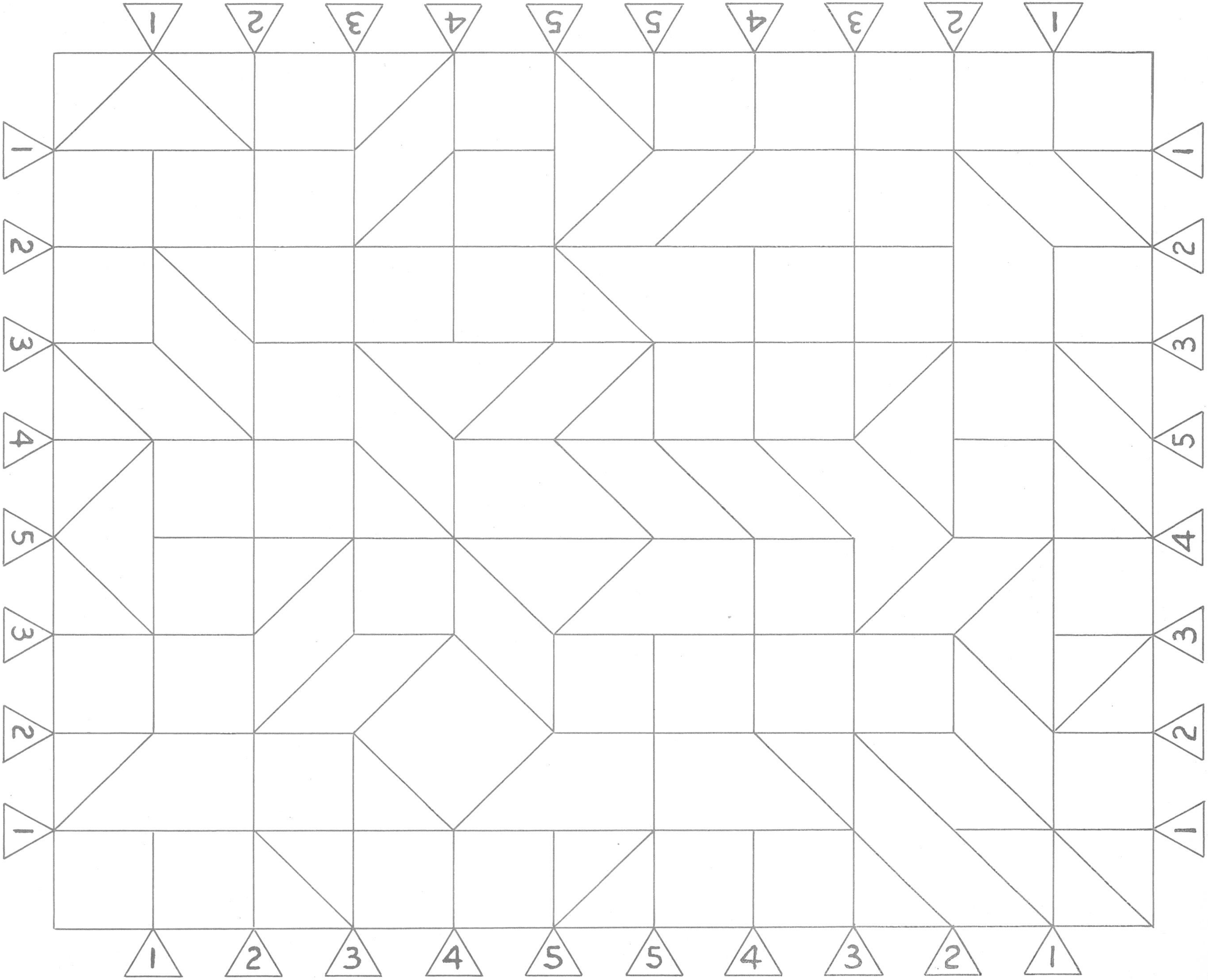

SPRINGER

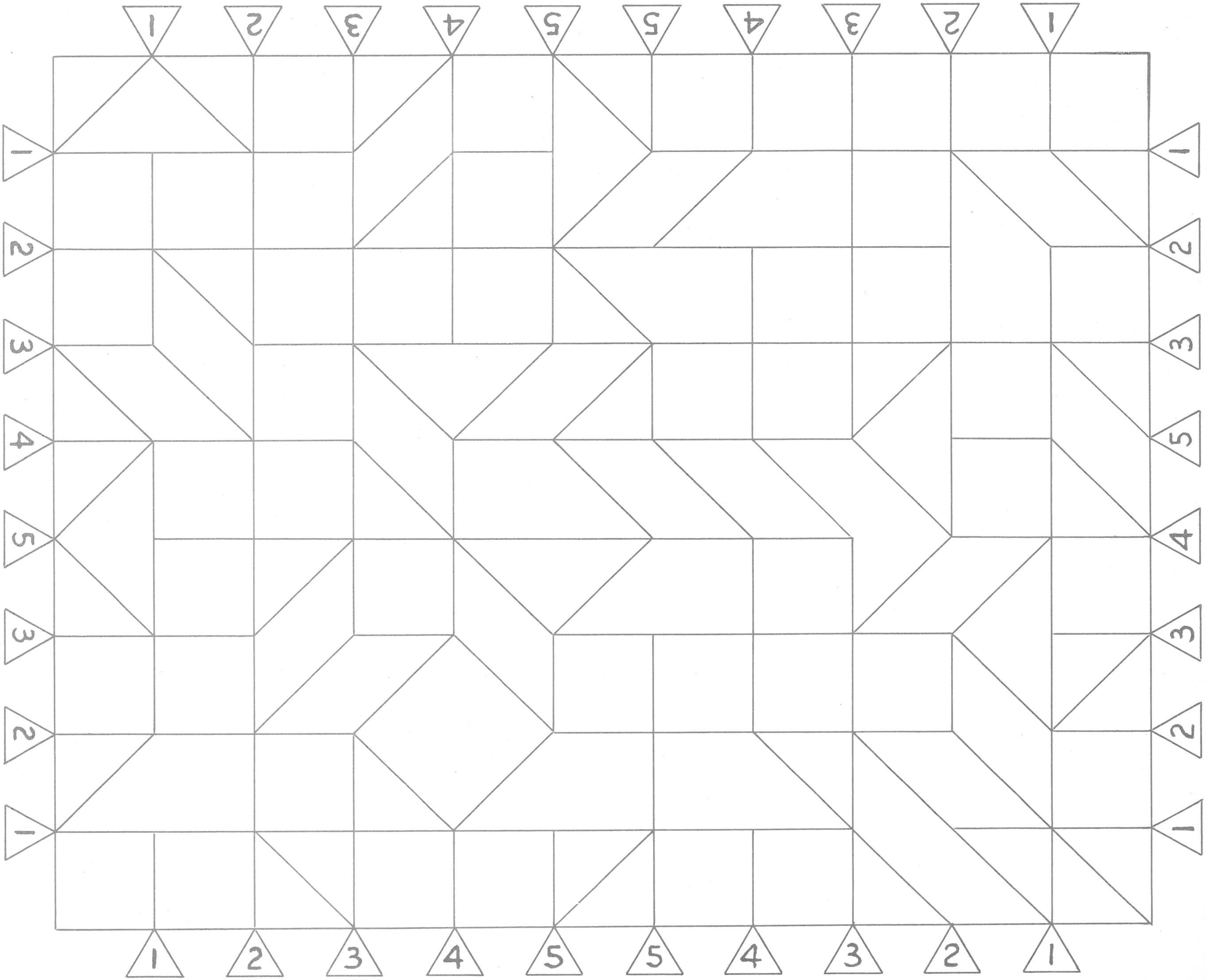

SPRINGER

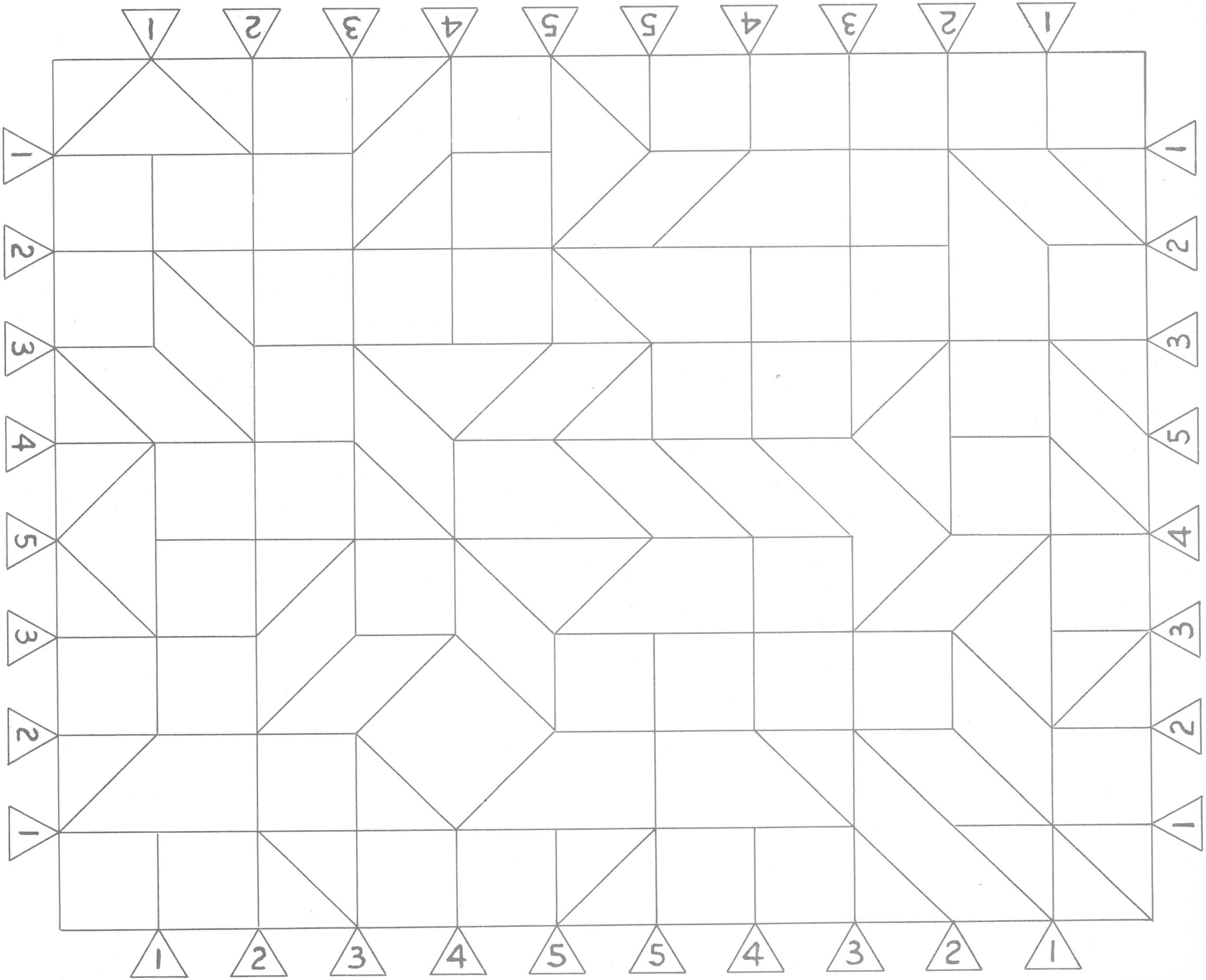

SPRINGER

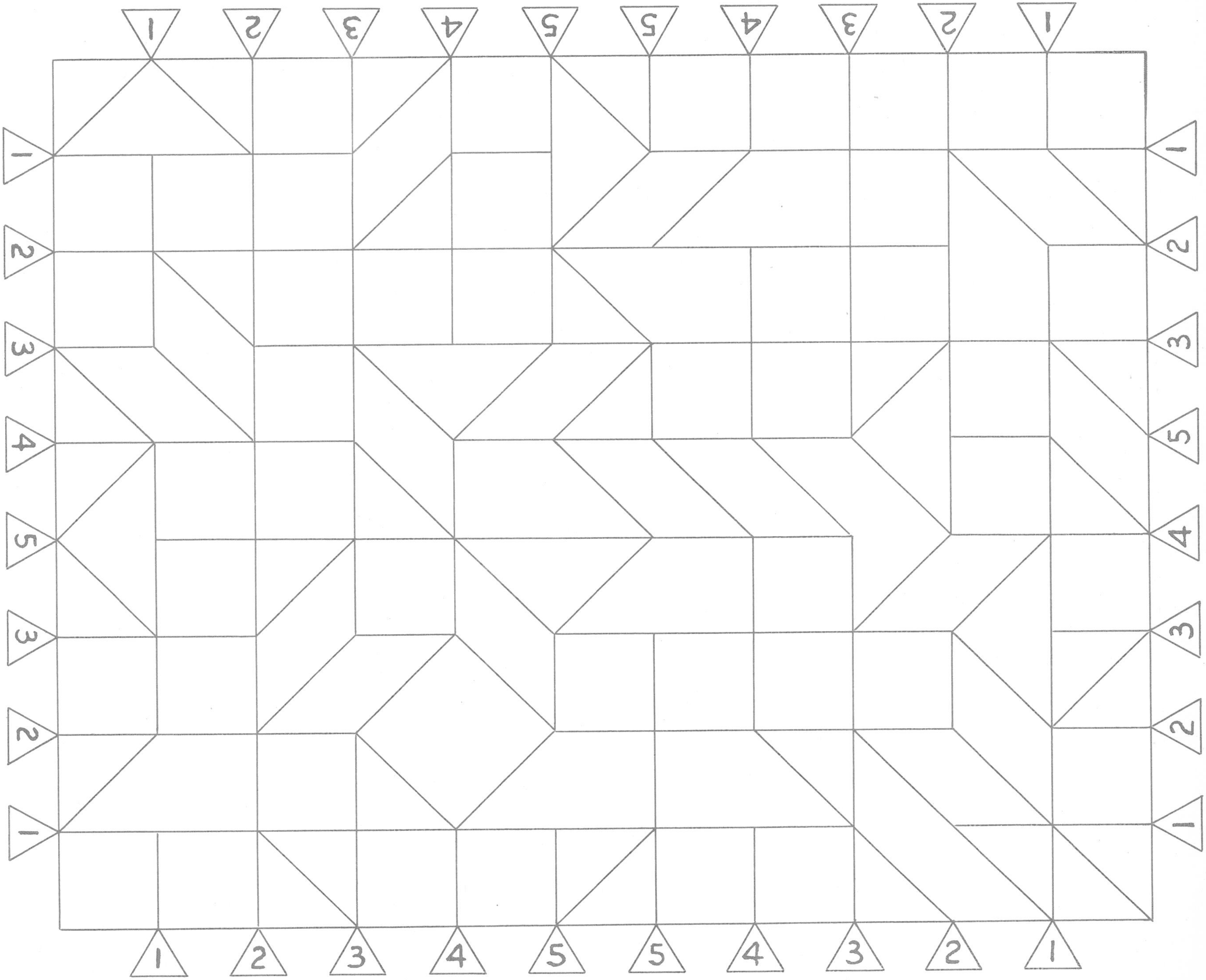

SPRINGER

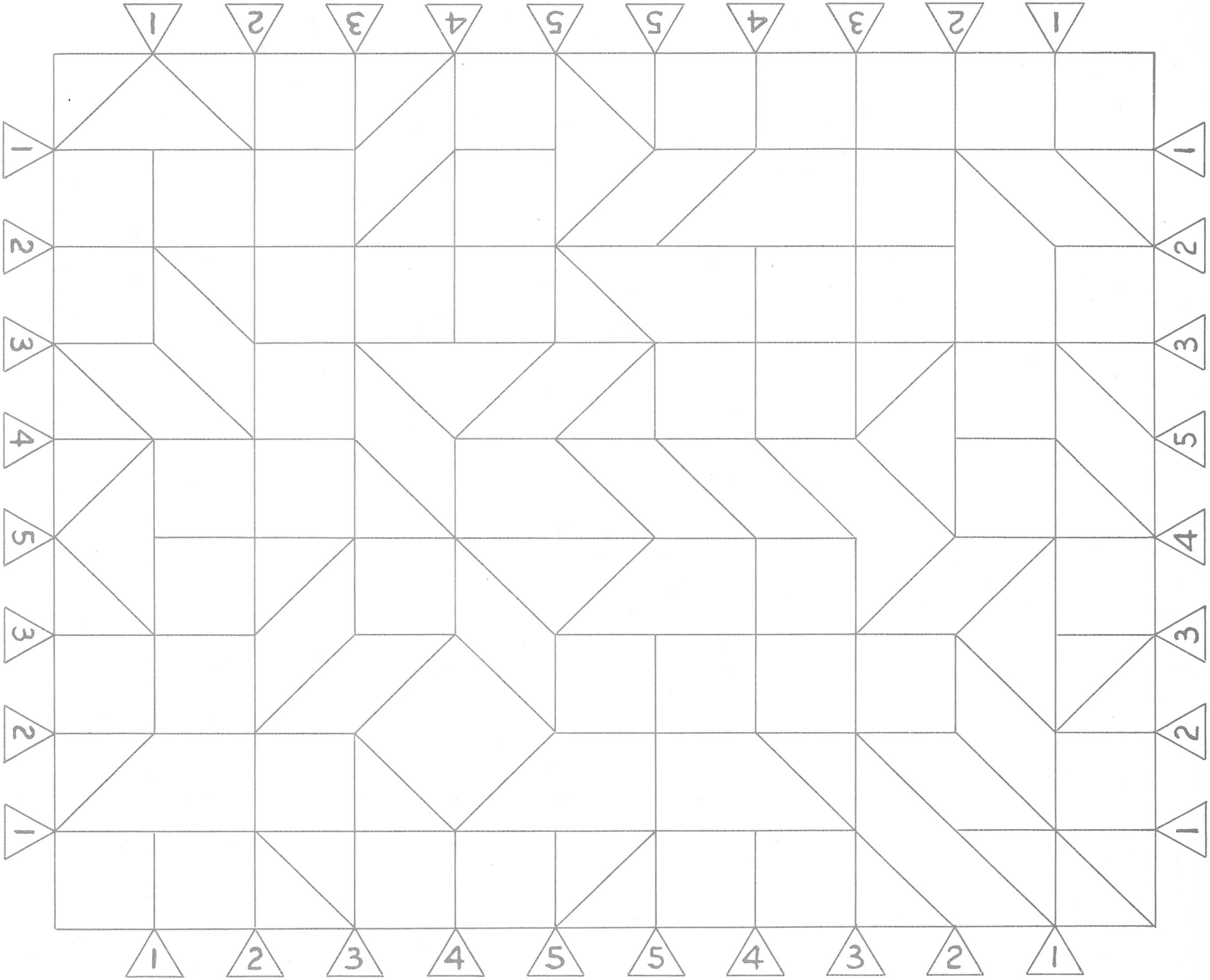

SPRINGER